A Different Kind of Teacher

A practical guide to the understanding and resolving of personal, interpersonal, student and classroom management difficulties within the school.

Tony Humphreys, B.A., H.D.E., M.A., Ph. D.

Consultant Clinical Psychologist in Private Practice and Specialist Lecturer for Health Care Professions and Teachers at University College, Cork, University College, Dublin and Mary Immaculate College of Education, Limerick.

First Edition 1993
© **1993 Tony Humphreys**

ISBN Number: 1-898207-00 -3

Published by: **Dr. Tony Humphreys**

Printed by: **Carraig Print**
                    Carrigtwohill,
                    Cork, Ireland.

Cover Design: **Mr. Liam Nott**

For Helen

ACKNOWLEDGEMENTS

The people I most want to acknowledge are all the primary and second-level teachers who came to my courses, revealing their needs and challenging my responses to them. I am also indebted to the individual teachers and students who during therapy provided me with insights into school and classroom systems.

A special thanks to Mr. Tony Doyle, Director of In-service, in Mary Immaculate College of Education, Limerick, who initiated and organised the two courses I now run there on an annual basis.

I am especially grateful to Anita Carney for her skill, patience and cheerfulness in preparing the different drafts of this book.

A special thank you to my partner Helen who was the sounding-board for many of my ideas and who with her sister, Svada Ruddle, helped in the proof-reading of this book.

TABLE OF CONTENTS

INTRODUCTION

Recent research in education has revealed that 'how' a teacher teaches is as important as 'what' he or she teaches.

Indeed, the 'how' largely determines effectiveness. The 'how' is related to the teacher's level of self-esteem and the ability, or lack of it, to form close relationships with students. The 'how' also involves awareness and practise of positive classroom management approaches. Furthermore, individual teacher's effectiveness is enhanced by a whole-school management style and by effective leadership within the school system. It is pertinent that research indicates that the three sources of stress in teaching are role load, staff relationships and difficult students. Research also indicates that the effects of role load are considerably reduced where there is strong staff cohesiveness and co-operation. Also, the teacher who has high self-esteem complains far less of discipline problems than the teacher with middle or poor self-esteem. These observations have been substantiated by findings that the effective school is characterised by high expectations, emotional responsiveness and effective leadership. High expectations mean believing in each student's ability to learn and emphasis being placed on effort rather than performance. Responsiveness involves a democratic caring approach to students with an emphasis on students taking responsibility for themselves.

Following on the research evidence but, principally, on my own personal experiences of teaching at primary and second-level schools and currently at third level, my involvement with teaching staffs over several years and my therapeutic work with teachers and others suffering personal, interpersonal and occupational conflicts, this book focuses on eight main areas:

- Stress Management
- Self-Esteem of Teachers
- Staff Relationships and Morale
- Self-Esteem of Students
- Emotional and Behavioural Problems of Students and Staff
- Classroom Management

- Whole-School Approach
- Effective Leadership

WHO THIS BOOK IS FOR

This book is particularly aimed at primary and second-level school teachers but it has relevance to anybody in education where there is teacher-student, teacher-teacher and leader-teacher relationships. It is also relevant to policy-makers as it provides insights into the needs of students, teachers, principals, vice-principals, parents, and others within school systems. The book offers considerable insights to parents on the nature of the problems their children may be experiencing in school. It also apprises parents of how to create a positive environment for learning within the home.

This book is for all students in the education profession and at all levels: in basic training, at diploma, graduate and post-graduate levels. It is also of use to lecturers in education.

WHAT IS IN THE BOOK

The book is divided into six chapters, each chapter focusing on a distinct area relevant to the development of more effective teaching.

Chapter one discusses the teaching profession and why and how it has become more highly stressed. It looks at the nature of stress, how to identify the signs of stress and how to cope and develop personally and professionally from it.

The second chapter focuses on the teacher with particular emphasis on self-esteem. It identifies three levels of self-esteem and outlines its effects on the person himself or herself and on students and colleagues. It introduces the reader to two communication patterns, introjection and projection, which are revelations of self-esteem problems and have serious effects on relationships within the classroom and staffroom. Most of all this chapter shows how self-esteem can be changed.

The next and longest chapter in this book is given over to the staffroom, a source of much stress for many teachers. Staff relationships, effective communication patterns, staff morale, staff affirmation, responding to rigidity in oneself, principals or colleagues and problem-solving are all discussed.

The focus of the fourth chapter is on the student. The early part of the chapter helps teachers to understand the nature of students' emotional, social and behavioural problems within the school and classroom and how to effectively respond to their manifestation. Particular emphasis is placed on students' self-esteem, how to identify problematic self-esteem and how to raise the level of a student's self-esteem. The effects of students' self-esteem on motivation and learning are also illustrated.

The fifth chapter attends to the classroom. It distinguishes between problems of over-control and under-control in students and how the latter cause the greatest disruption in class, even though the former are indicators of a more at-risk pupil. The chapter also outlines behaviours on the part of the teacher that can precipitate problematic responses from students. It outlines essential aspects of effective classroom management, the design and implementation of effective systems of responsibility for students and the positive use of sanctions. There is a separate section given over to responding to the student who is recalcitrant.

The final chapter talks about the school and discusses such issues as what factors make for an effective school, a whole-school approach, effective leadership, coping styles within schools, parent -teacher liaison and school ethos. This chapter particularly confronts the need for shared responsibility and the need for confrontation by teachers of many of the issues within school systems that need to be altered. It also recommends the development of confidential counselling services for teachers and principals.

HOW TO USE THIS BOOK

The emphasis throughout the book is on five issues:
- Personal effectiveness
- Development of self-esteem enhancing relationships within the staffroom and classroom

- Creation of a greater insight into, understanding of and positive responding to the emotional, behavioural and social problems of students and teachers.
- Positive approaches to teaching
- Shared responsibility

The aim is always practical. The book includes examples of problematic situations within staffrooms and classrooms and case-studies I have encountered and offers tried and tested ways of resolving such conflicts. This book has principally developed from the many problems staff groups have presented to me during staff in-service days and our attempts at effective responses to those issues. At the end of each chapter there is a list of the key issues and key tasks that will lead to more effective personal, interpersonal and classroom management.

A good idea is to read the book through so that you get an overall view of the themes and practices recommended. On the other hand, you may like to turn to a chapter or sections on issues that currently concern you. Each chapter can stand on its own as it describes and discusses specific insights and skills. You can easily dip into particular sections within chapters.

The book could also be usefully employed by a staff group or a group of teachers to systematically work through in order to establish greater school effectiveness.

I hope you will find this book helpful in resolving many of the difficulties that are present within the teaching profession.

During the last nine years of my working with staff groups and giving courses to teacher groups, I have witnessed and been impressed by, and indeed overawed, at the commitment, dedication and 'need to know more' of teachers.

Finally, references to problems encountered with staff groups and case-studies have been sufficiently masked so that anonymity is ensured.

Tony Humphreys
CORK, IRELAND.

CHAPTER ONE

The Teaching Profession

1. THE NATURE OF STRESS

2. SIGNS OF STRESS

3. TEACHER STRESS

4. TEACHER 'BURNOUT'

5. COPING WITH STRESS

   - Balanced Life-style

   - Healthy Diet

   - Physical Fitness

   - Relaxation

6. KEY ISSUES

7. KEY TASKS

1. THE NATURE OF STRESS

Stress is a relatively new word for human problems in living. The word has been borrowed from the field of technology and it means 'pressure' or 'strain'. The effects of stress on a population's health are very high. It is reckoned that over two-thirds of office visits to general practitioners are due to stress related problems. The six leading causes of death - heart disease, cancer, cirrhosis of the liver, lung ailments, accidental injuries and suicide - are all directly or indirectly caused by stress. The three best-selling drugs are Valium which is a tranquilliser, Idera which is for hypertension (blood pressure) and Tagamet which is for ulcers and other stomach problems.

It is important to distinguish between what I call **necessary** and **emergency** stress. Necessary stress occurs, for example, when you eat and you put your digestive system under stress, or when you run or play games you put your cardiovascular system under stress or in preparing for a lecture a certain amount of apprehension pushes adrenalin into your system, mobilises your intellectual resources, increases concentration and motivation. However, if you over-eat or over-exercise or over-worry about a seminar presentation so that your stomach is in a knot, your heart racing and you feel pressure in your head you are now into 'emergency' stress. The word 'emergency' is very accurate because once you go beyond a certain level of stress you are in an 'emergency' state and some things need to be done to return you to a welfare state. So, for example, a typical cause of stress is the daily hassles of rushing and racing, meeting deadlines, attempting to do too many things at once and so on. If you go into many houses at half-past eight in the morning you will understand the stressful effects of daily hassles. People rush, race, choke back food, shout, roar, argue, make mistakes, can not remember and generally are as 'high as a kite'. Their bodies will now reveal the pressure they are putting themselves under; tension headaches, stomach 'butterflies', heart palpitations and other signs. The 'emergency' to be responded to is the rushing, racing, worrying by counter-behaviours of getting-up earlier, doing things calmly and thinking positively.

If these corrective behaviours are effective then one will return to a welfare state; if not, then the true causes of the emergency stress have not yet been isolated and further analysis is needed. Certainly a wise course of action for everybody is to learn to live in the present moment. Few people do. Since beginning this section of the book how many times has your mind wandered into the past or out into the future? The skill of present moment living is to focus totally on the action of the moment, whether it is reading a particular word or peeling a potato or listening to someone etc. Some readers will no doubt say "you have to think about the future and past". Planning for the future is, indeed, important but then planning is a present moment activity. Worrying about what is going to happen is a future activity and totally redundant. It is to be recommended you get into the habit of simple time management, to plan your day, week, month, or year ahead. Time-management ensures allocation of time for all your essential needs. The more you meet your different needs the less you are stressed. It is important to learn from the past but not to live in it as many people do by regretting, bemoaning, complaining and comparing. Evaluation is a present moment activity of bringing the benefit of experience to bear on present moment activity.

2. SIGNS OF STRESS

It is not too difficult to determine your level of stress. Below is a list of the main signs of stress. Go carefully through them and underline any symptom you experience. It would also be wise to ask yourself how frequently and to what degree of intensity (hardly noticeable to very debilitating) you experience the underlined symptoms. Also check how long have you had the symptom.

Signs of Stress

1. **Emotional Signs**
    Anxiety, aggression, apathy, boredom, depression, fatigue, frustration, guilt and shame, irritability and bad temper,

moodiness, low self-esteem, threat and tension, nervousness, loneliness and hypersensitivity to criticism.

2. **Behavioural Signs**

Accident proneness, drug taking, temper outbursts, excessive eating or loss of appetite, excessive drinking and smoking, excitability, impulsive behaviour, impaired speech, nervous laughter, restlessness, trembling, rushing, doing too many things at the one time.

3. **Cognitive Signs**

Inability to make decisions and concentrate, frequent forgetfulness, negative thinking, mental blocks, living in the past or future.

4. **Body Effects**

Increased heart rate and blood pressure, dryness of mouth, sweating, dilation of pupils, difficulty in breathing, hot and cold spells, a 'lump in the throat', numbness and tingling in parts of the limbs, stomach butterflies.

5. **Health Effects**

Asthma, amenorrhoea, chest and back pains, coronary heart disease, diarrhoea, faintness and dizziness, dyspepsia, frequent urination, headaches and migraine, neuroses, nightmares, insomnia, psychoses, psychosomatic disorder, diabetes mellitus, skin rash, ulcers, loss of sexual interest and weakness.

6. **School Effects**

Absenteeism, poor staff relations, and poor motivation, high staff turnover rates, poor staff morale, antagonism at work and job dissatisfaction.

In going through the above list if you did not underline any of the symptoms please consult a clinical psychologist or psychotherapist immediately as you are into what is massive 'denial'. There is no one without some degree of emergency stress! If you underlined most of the signs pick up the phone immediately for a consultation!

Be wary of jumping to conclusions when you experience any one or more of the above symptoms. People tend to think the worst so that a persistent headache becomes a sign of a brain tumor, a pain in the chest a sure indicator of heart disease and a discomfiture in the stomach becomes a cancer. The difficulty is that such an alarmist response shoots stress levels up much higher so that symptoms increase in intensity, which in turn convinces you of your catastrophic diagnosis, so that the spiralling of panic continues to escalate. It reminds me of a teacher who came up to me at the end of lecture and told me he had been experiencing for five years three of the symptoms on the stress signs checklist given above. The three symptoms were dryness of the mouth, lower back pain and frequent urination. He had been to a number of medical consultants over the years but no one could explain why he had the symptoms. Nevertheless, he was prescribed pain killers for his back, a spray for his mouth but nothing for the frequent urination. Despite the medical treatments the symptoms had not abated over the five years. Indeed, at times, they severely escalated. It is always wise to get yourself physically checked out, particularly for some persistent physical symptom. However, when you get a clear bill of physical health, then you need to look at possible psychological and social causes of the symptoms. This particular teacher did not do the latter. What he did do was to convince himself that he had cancer and he believed the doctors were either not really telling him or that they had not discovered it. To go around believing you have cancer is extremely frightening and highly stressful and it was no wonder that the stress symptoms had not abated. What often triggers stress is change. I asked this teacher had something changed in his life five years before - did somebody close to him die, did he get married, were there marital problems, a new addition to the family, in-laws coming to live-in, loss of status etc. It was really quite simple; five years before he had taken over the principalship of a large secondary school. It was then the symptoms became apparent. He was very dependent on others for acceptance and approval, had a dread of failure and generally was a worrier. He would always have been under a certain level of stress owing to these underlying vulnerabilities. The extra responsibilities heightened the risk of failure and disapproval and his underlying fears now became heightened and more apparent. The man's problem was certainly not cancer, nor was it lower back pain, dryness of mouth or frequent urination nor the change to school principalship but his long-term vulnerabilities of fears, dependency and low self-esteem. When these latter were corrected the symptoms which had so scared him disappeared.

Stress is Positive!

Bear in mind that emergency stress is positive! It alerts you to change that is needed in some area of your life; it may be within yourself (self- esteem), it may be interpersonal indicating the need for change in some important relationship, it may be professional, the need for change within some aspect of your work or, in some cases, a total career change. The possibilities are endless. Each person has to find the source of his or her own stress. If necessity is the mother of invention then stress can be the father of self-actualisation.

3. TEACHER STRESS

Stress in teaching has been getting a fair degree of press in recent years. The number of people wanting to get out of the profession is high and the number going into it is lower. The rise in early retirement on the basis of health grounds is unprecedented. What has happened to bring about these changes? Occupational stress is a function of two main factors: demands and control. When demands in an occupation are high and control is low you have a high stress job. A low stress position is the opposite: demands are low and control is high. Air traffic controllers have high-stress work because demands on them are very high as the least mistake may cause a major disaster and control is minimal as air space is taken up very quickly, particularly in the busy airports in the world.

Librarians, on the other hand, have low demands made on them and they have high control over the rate at which they work. There has been a double shift in these factors within the teaching profession. Within the last two decades the role demands on teachers have increased enormously and control (discipline) issues have become a major problem for many schools. The combination of increased demands and control difficulties has moved teaching into a high stress occupation. There are differences between schools but all schools will have experienced some increase in stress levels. A research study carried out in the Mid-Western area of Ireland distinguished between advantaged (middle-class) schools and disadvantaged (more lower/working class) schools. The study surveyed the prevalence of educational, behavioural and emotional problems of primary school children. In the advantaged schools at least ten per cent of children had serious behavioural and emotional difficulties; in the disadvantaged areas the percentage was considerably higher at twenty seven per cent. Little or no psychological or social back-up services are available to these schools and teachers, who though not trained to understand or cope with these difficulties, are nonetheless expected to do so. Such children present many control difficulties within the classroom and, not surprisingly, one of the major causes of teacher stress is students with emotional and behavioural problems. Inadequate classroom and whole-school management systems, or resortment to old destructive authoritarian methods serve only to increase control difficulties. Ineffective leadership is another major contributor to stress in teaching as many principals, who may have been effective as teachers, do not lead well. The skills of teaching are very different to the skills of leadership and it is not a Department of Education policy that principals be required to do management courses. Lack of cohesiveness between leaders and staff makes for inconsistency and unpredictability in management of classrooms and the school. Consistency and predictability are the hallmarks of good management systems and their lack means many control difficulties. If control problems are increasing in schools so also are the demands made on teachers. These demands principally came from an educational system that has put the emphasis on performance in examinations as the main criterion for success. The competition for 'points' to get into a third level co seriously pressurised second-level educators into an educati philosophy that is discriminatory (students who are considere bright are more reinforced) and conditional (learning not for learning sake but for 'points' sake). All this is immensely taxing on teachers themselves as they tend to measure their professional effectiveness by examination results. What is even more worrying is that primary schools now view entrance examinations to secondary schools as a major goal and preparations begin in fifth class for this event. There is also an increase in inter-school competition measured by how many children get into the 'best' schools. Examinations only measure an aspect of academic development. To evaluate teaching purely on such a narrow criterion would do serious injustice to teachers who help poorly motivated children to develop from low levels of learning to moderate levels of learning. It is little credit to teachers who bring highly motivated students to high examination results. Yet the emphasis and appraisal tend to be on these latter students. Furthermore, education is not just about academic development. Surely of equal importance is the emotional, social, sexual, physical, behavioural, spiritual and creative development of children. Indeed, educational research is now showing that of primary importance is the emotional development of children in the classroom and school. Children with learning difficulties generally have low self-esteem and unless this emotional problem is corrected remedial efforts tend to have minimal effects. Marital breakdown, which is now quite widespread in Ireland, unemployment, profound social and political changes, the fall in religious practise, all serve to make more demands on teachers in classrooms. Bureaucracy and its obsessive need for paper-work makes for more demands, particularly on principals and vice-principals, who very often, because of cut-backs, do not have any secretarial assistance. Many principals are also under pressure because of demoralisation among their teaching staff. The fact that the profession is not a well-paid one and that promotion is limited does not help matters.

...stress have become known as 'burn-
...out are listed below:

...under or over-eating)

- ...mplaints (eg. headaches, back pain, chest
pain, s... ...oblems, bowel problems).
- Irritability
- Reliance on drugs such as alcohol, tranquillisers, anti-
depressants, nicotine.
- Pessimism and fatalism
- Increasing discouragement
- Negative attitudes to teaching and to students
- Poor relationships with colleagues
- Loss of self-esteem
- Loss of motivation to develop oneself
- Reduced involvement in life
- Loss of creativity

Again, in checking through this list, evaluate the frequency, intensity and duration of the symptoms.

Occupational burnout is rarely a product purely of the job
itself. Generally, it is a combination of personal vulnerability and
occupational stress that brings about burnout. A case history will
bring this point home. This was a teacher who had been teaching
for fifteen years. In the year prior to coming to see me she had got
an extremely difficult leaving certificate examination class. This
teacher was very dependent on academic results as a measure of her
worth as a person. This dependency made her hypersensitive to any
criticism or disapproval and, certainly, failure in terms of poor academic results highly threatened her self-esteem. Consequently, she
worked tooth and nail to bring this class up to 'her standards'. She
was under constant strain during the year. At the end of the
academic year she was emotionally drained and physically ex-

hausted and rather than sighing with relief that the year was over and she could now enjoy the three best things about teaching, June, July and August, she now worried what would the examination results reveal. When the results came out in August the 'difficult' class did quite well and now rather than clapping herself on the back for a job well done, she worried and fretted that if she got another class like that in September she would not be able to cope. By the time September came she had immobilised herself with fear and was unable to return to school. When she came to see me in mid-October absenteeism was total - she had not returned to school at all. There were dark circles under her eyes revealing physical exhaustion, insomnia and loss of appetite. She was on both anti-depressants and tranquillisers. She complained of severe head-aches and nausea. She felt she could no longer cope with teaching and students. Her discouragement was total and her loss of self-esteem was serious as she now saw herself as 'a total failure'. She was utterly pessimistic and fatalistic about the future and her motivation and involvement in life had totally plummeted. She sat around most of the time brooding about her problems which served only to increase them.

The above description is typical of many teachers I have helped over the years. This teacher's burnout resulted from both her own poor self-esteem with accompanying dependency and multiple fears and the increased pressure from the difficult examination class. The help that is needed in such cases is of personal empowerment in terms of self-esteem elevation and independence of others and of performance and more constructive approaches to teaching and, whenever possible, development of a supportive and dynamic staffroom environment (more about this later). When these or at least some of these issues are resolved the stressed teacher returns to his/her work.

5. COPING WITH STRESS

As has been seen **stress is positive** as it indicates the need for change. Furthermore, each person has to detect the source(s) of his or her own stress and on discovery take corrective actions. Nevertheless, there are coping actions that help all people under stress even though they rarely resolve the underlying issue(s) unique to each person's stress problems. Stress management clinics have mushroomed all over America and they are beginning also to appear in this country. These clinics tend to focus on four main coping skills:

- **Balanced Life-Style**
- **Healthy Diet**
- **Physical Exercise**
- **Relaxation**

• Balanced Life-Style

I have already alluded to this coping mechanism. Many people referred with stress-related diseases like heart disease, ulcers, back pain, etc. typically present with imbalanced life styles. I remember about ten years ago lecturing to a group of medical doctors on the wonders of clinical hypnosis. At the end of the presentation I sat down to take questions and my lower back went into spasm. The pain was excruciating and through clenched teeth I cancelled the questions. How embarassing! there was I heralding the wonders of clinical hypnosis and then I collapsed with psychosomatic pain. They were all medical doctors and they wanted to cart me off to hospital. However, I knew what the problem was. I persuaded them to get me down onto the carpeted floor and inject the muscle concerned with a muscle relaxant. However, the spasm had gone too far and could not be controlled. Eventually, I had them slide me into the back seat of my car, drive me to my home and put me to bed. I knew the only answer was bed rest. Here was a loud 'emergency' signal for me. Indeed, I had been getting twinges of pain for sometime but had ignored them. When the symptom is ignored it has to get louder in order to alert the person to the stress being created and the changes that are needed. The very apparent cause of the lower back pain was overwork. At the time I was spending between 70 to 80 hours weekly between therapy and lecturing. I took the advice of developing a more balanced life-style and began to time-manage all my major personal, interpersonal and professional needs. I also resurrected my ability to self-hypnotise and to breathe diaphragmatically. I delegated more work to colleagues, took up tennis and walking to strengthen my body, took much more care of my diet and planned regular holidays. All in all it was a commendable effort to reduce my stress levels. Did it work? Certainly, for six months I maintained the effort and I had no reoccurence of the severe pain. However, after six months I found myself increasing my workload. Clearly, I had not got to the bottom of my compulsion to overwork. A question I would have needed to ask myself six months previously was "why am I over working?". Certainly the imbalanced life-style due to the long working hours was the surface reason for my emergency stress level but a much deeper reason had yet to be dealt with and failure to deal with it explained the gradual return to old neglectful ways. The answer to the question was an inability to say 'no' to people who needed help or made requests of me. This non-assertiveness was due to my identity being tied up with being the helper. As a child my mother was wheel-chair bound and it was I who mostly looked after her and the other members of the family. Relatives and others used to say "what a marvellous child" who can cook, shop, clean the house and take care of his mother. To say 'no' would subconsciously mean losing this regard and becoming invisible in the eyes of others. Such is the effect of a conditional upbringing. Now I can say 'no', not all of the time, but much of the time. I have learned that my identity is separate from what I do and that my needs deserve as much consideration as do the needs of others. Inevitably, people with self-esteem problems are neglectful of many of their essential needs. It requires considerable discipline to correct this imbalance and the best approach is through simple time-management so that you ensure that at least most of your essential needs are met within any one couple of days. Each need area deserves to be responded to and so check the following list and see how well and how often you meet them:

- **Emotional** needs of love, affection, warmth, closeness, support, understanding, compassion, challenge, humour.

- **Cognitive** needs of intellectual stimulation, reading, discussion, challenge, problem solving, responsibility.

- **Behavioural** needs for the development of a whole range of skills - cooking, painting, dressing, writing, car maintenance, gardening, woodwork.

- **Social** needs for friendship, companionship, sharing of expertise and knowledge.

- **Physical** needs for health, fitness, comfort, safety, food and warmth.

- **Sensual** needs so that the five senses receive adequate stimulation.

- **Occupational** needs for meaningful work, fair salary, good conditions, recognition for input, staff cohesiveness and support, benefit systems, promotional opportunities. .

- **Sexual** needs for gratification of sexual drive within the context of a mature and loving relationship.

- **Recreational** needs for rest, games, sports, hobbies, interests.

- **Spiritual** needs for transcendence, mystical experiences and meaningful explanation for existence.

Remember if you fail to keep to a balanced life-style then there is some deeper issue that needs to be detected and a deeper level of responding is needed.

• Healthy Diet

Your energy is maintained by three main sources: sleep, food and fitness. Food to be beneficial needs to be nourishing. Also, it is important that your diet follows your energy pattern. Many books on diet suggest that breakfast is the most important meal of the day. My body does not agree with that suggestion. Following a night's sleep my energy is high and I do not feel particularly hungry. I am a great believer in listening to what my body says. So, in the morning I tend to have a light breakfast of fresh orange juice, two slices of brown bread, and a cup of coffee. However, come lunchtime, after working some four or five hours, my body sends messages of starvation and I tend to eat my main meal of the day at lunchtime. If I do not respond to my low energy levels, expressed through hunger, I find by mid-afternoon I am drowsy and headachy. However, when I eat a good wholesome meal I find I can continue to work up to 7.00p.m. without any symptoms of fatigue. By that time I am hungry again and I will eat again but not a big meal as at lunchtime. It is unfortunate that many professionals have made lunch what I call 'a banana and yoghurt affair' and that their main meal is eaten in the evening when as much energy will not be needed to complete the day's activities.

The important issue regarding diet is to avoid junk foods which have no energy value. Most packaged foods have taken the good out of food; regrettably, most 'convenience' food is pack-aged. It is best to avoid packaged food and eat as much fresh foods as possible. One further issue is not to use food as a substitute for other needs like love, comfort, warmth and support or not to use food as a means of reducing fear. Both of these latter responses to unmet needs only create another problem which is overeating and obesity.

• Physical Fitness

It is known that people who are physically fit withstand the physio-logical effects of stress more that those who are physically unfit. Commonsense, you may say, but it always puzzles me why they called good sense commonsense as it tends to be a very rare commodity indeed! 'Raresense' would be a more accurate descrip-tive word. It does not take too much to establish physical fitness but what it does take is regularity. Thirty to forty minutes, four or five times weekly, of a moderate type exercise like walking, swimming, tennis, cycling, is all that is required. Weekend athleticism is of little or no use. Furthermore, be sure you perspire when you exercise, otherwise you may only be 'dawdling' which is not physical exercise of a worthwhile nature. Do not exercise beyond tiredness or exhaustion as this is overstressing your body and, if done regularly, puts you at risk. Many keep-fit fanatics suffer early disease or death as extreme exercising is an abuse of one's physical system and leads to eventual physical breakdown. If in reading this section you have been thinking 'where in the name of all that is holy am I going to find thirty to forty minutes, four or five times weekly', please return to the previous section on balanced life-style.

Again, routine helps in the establishment of an exercise regime. Be flexible in your routine as rigid adherence to any behaviour has its own inbuilt stressor.

● Relaxation

There is evidence that regular practice of relaxation can add considerably to one's life span. Relaxation, to my mind, is an essential requisite for all teachers. One of my recommendations to teachers is, that no matter how disruptive, aggressive, uncooperative students are, stay totally calm and unflappable. It is important that students perceive that their irresponsible behaviour has no control over you. If you lose your cool in the face of their problematic behaviours they will be quick to spot this weakness and exploit it for their own needs to be maladaptively met within a classroom. Furthermore, a teacher needs at all times to model self-control and by staying relaxed and calm but firm, the teacher exhibits the control (s)he expects of students in the classroom and school corridors. However, if in teaching you shout and roar (out-of-control behaviour) to gain control of a class, students again are quick to see the hypocrisy of this demand and may not respond to your negative overtures for responsibility on their part. There is a far greater likelihood that matters will deescalate if the teacher remains calm and relaxed.

Relaxation is a skill that needs practice, just like driving a car, playing golf, and playing the piano. It is necessary to know that relaxation is not resting. Curled up in front of a glowing fire, with a brandy and the Late Late Show on T.V., is resting but not relaxation. Relaxation is a deeper experience and stretches from light, medium to deep and trance level responses. At the beginning of training oneself it is good to practise an exercise twice daily for 10 to 15 minutes at a time. I have included a five minute exercise and a tension releasing exercise at the end of this section but I would recommend attending some relaxation classes for more indepth understanding and experience of relaxation. The aim is to eventually be able to bring the relaxation response into all life situations, and most particularly stressful situations like conflict incidences within classrooms or staffrooms. There are many types of relaxation methods, Yoga, Transcendental Meditation, Progressive Muscular Relaxation, Hypnosis, Autogenics, Visualisation, etc. Different methods suit different people. If you have a vivid imagination use visualisation methods, if you are more interested in physical activity, then muscular relaxation or yoga might suit and if you have retained trance ability from childhood then hypnotic approaches would be desirable. Relaxation is a lifetime skill that everyone needs to develop, most of all adults who have the charge of the mature development of children.

The above described four coping mechanisms are a good starting point in establishing a positive life-style cycle. When these mechanisms become a routine part of your behavioural repertoire you are then in a better position to begin to explore deeper levels of change that may be needed in your personal, interpersonal and professional life.

Quick Release of Tension Exercise

Whenever you feel anxious, panicky or uptight ....

1.   Let your breath go (don't breathe in first).
2.   Take in a slow, gentle breath; hold it for a second.
3.   Let it go, with a leisurely sigh of relief.
4.   Drop your shoulders at the same time and relax your hands.

5.   Make sure your teeth are not clenched together.
6.   If you have to speak, speak more slowly and in a lower tone
     of voice.

Short Relaxation Exercise

This exercise is for when you have only a short time to spare. It is
better to have a chair with arms, but ideally, you should be able to
learn to relax anywhere you find yourself. Use a cushion in the
small of the back if it helps. Make sure you are warm.

Sit upright and well back in the chair so that your thighs and
back are supported, and rest your hand in the cradle position on
your lap, or lightly on top on your thighs. If you like, take off your
shoes, and let your feet rest on the ground (if they don't touch the
floor, try and find a book or similar object to rest them on). If you
want to, close your eyes.

Begin by breathing out first. Then breathe in easily, just as
much as you need Now breath out slowly, with a slight sigh, like
a balloon slowly deflating. Do this once more, slowly .... breathe
in ..... breathe out ..... as you breathe out, feel the tension begin to
drain away. Then go back to your ordinary breathing, even, quiet,
steady.

Now direct your thoughts to each part of your body in turn, to
the muscles and joints.

Think first about your left foot. Your toes are still. Your foot
feels heavy on the floor. Let your foot and toes start to feel
completely relaxed.

Now think about your right foot ... toes .... ankles .... they are
resting heavily on the floor. Let both your feet, your toes, ankles
start to relax.

Now think about your legs. Let your legs feel completely relaxed
and heavy on the chair. Your thighs, your knees roll outwards when
they relax, so let them go.

Think now about your back, and your spine. Let the tension
drain away, from your back, and from your spine. Follow your
breathing, and each time you breathe out, relax your back and
spine a little more.

Let your abdominal muscles become soft and loose. There's no need to hold your stomach in tight, it rises and falls as you breathe quietly - feel that your stomach is completely relaxed.

No tension in your chest. Let your breathing be slow and easy, and each time you breathe out, let it go a little more.

Think now about the fingers of your left hand - they are curved, limp and quite still. Now the fingers of your right hand .....relaxed ..... soft and still. Let this feeling of relaxation spread ..... up your arms ..... feel the heaviness in your arms ...... up to your shoulders. Let your shoulders relax, let them drop easily ...... and then let them drop even further than you thought they could.Think about your neck. Feel the tension melt away from your neck and shoulders. Each time you breathe out, relax your neck a little more.

Now before we move on, just check to see if all these parts of your body are still relaxed - your feet, legs, back and spine, stomach, hands, arms, neck and shoulders. Keep your breathing gentle and easy. Every time you breathe out, relax a little more and let all the tensions ease away from your body. No tensions - just enjoy this feeling of relaxation.

Now think about your face. Let the expression come off your face. Smooth out your brow, and let your forehead feel wide and relaxed. Let your eyebrows drop gently. There is no tension around your eyes - your eyelids slightly closed, your eyes are still. Let your jaw unwind - teeth slightly apart as your jaw unwinds more and more.

Feel the relief of letting go.

Now think about your tongue and throat. Let your tongue drop down to the bottom of your mouth and relax completely. Relax your tongue and throat. And your lips slightly parted, no pressure between them.Let all the muscles in your face unwind and let go - there is no tension in your face - just let it relax more and more.

Now, instead of thinking about yourself in parts, feel the all-over sensation of letting go, of quiet and of rest. Check to see if you are still relaxed. Stay like this for a few moments, and listen to your breathing .... in ....and out .... let your body become looser, heavier, each time you breathe out.

Now continue for a little longer, and enjoy this time for relaxation.

Coming back - slowly, move your hands a little and your feet. When you are ready, open your eyes and sit quiet for a while. Stretch, if you want to, or yawn, and slowly start to move again.

6. KEY ISSUES

The foregoing section on stress and stress in teaching have highlighted the following issues:
● The distinction between 'necessary' and 'emergency' stress.
● The recognition of stress by means of the symptoms checklist
● Be wary of 'denial' of stress experiences.
● Holistically evaluate a recurrent symptom - do not jump to the 'worst' conclusion.
● A life-event often triggers a stress response.
● Stress is positive; it alerts one to the need for change.
● Occupational stress is a function of high demands and low control.
● Multiple role demands, students with behavioural and emotional problems, staff relationships and ineffective leadership are the main sources of stress in teaching.
● Education is not just about academic development but also involves responding to the emotional, social, sexual, spiritual, behavioural and physical needs of each student.
Low self-esteem of students is the main contributor to poor academic functioning.
● Burnout in teachers arises from a combination of personal vulnerability and occupational stress.

7. KEY TASKS

The key actions recommended in the section under consideration were:
● Live in the present moment.
● Detect one's own stress symptoms.
● Identify one's own unique source(s) of stress.

- Practise coping mechanisms of:-
    - Balanced Life-style
    - Healthy Diet
    - Physical Fitness
    - Relaxation
- Keep calm and unflappable in the face of problematic behaviours in the classroom and staffroom.

CHAPTER TWO

The Teacher

1. **SELF-ESTEEM OF TEACHERS**

    A. Levels of Self-Esteem

    B. Origins of Self-Esteem

    C. Self-Esteem and Teaching

    D. Self-Esteem and Teacher Training

    E. Changing Self-Esteem

    - *Checklist for Self-Esteem Enhancement*

    - *Changing Communication Patterns*

        - Projection
        - Introjection

2. **KEY ISSUES**

3. **KEY TASKS**

1. SELF-ESTEEM OF TEACHERS

There are many personal and professional reasons why teachers need to look at the whole area of self-worth. Medical evidence shows a strong correlation between physical health and longevity and high self-esteem. Likewise psychiatry and psychology have shown that people's problems in living are related to personal vulnerability and feelings of inferiority. Family and marital well-being are strongly related to the high self-esteem of parents and partners.

Indeed, the well-being of all human systems is determined by the level of self-esteem of each of the participants of a particular system. Clearly, leaders have a higher responsibility to increase their self-esteem as problematic self-esteem leads to ineffective leadership. Finally, the teacher with high self-esteem produces students with high self-esteem and, sadly, the converse is also true.

What is self-esteem? Basically self-esteem has to do with how you feel about two aspects of yourself - lovability and capability. Many of the clients I work with state that they see nothing about themselves that is lovable, neither do they see themselves as being capable of doing anything. The perception often is totally contrary to the very obvious beauty, attractiveness, creativity, high intelligence and ability of the person.
Dorothy Corkille Briggs sums it up very well.

"A person's judgement of self influences the kind of friends he chooses, how he gets along with others, the kind of person he marries and how productive he will be. It affects his creativity, integrity, stability and even whether he will be a leader or a follower. His feeling of self-worth forms the core of his personality and determines the uses he makes of his aptitudes and abilities. His attitude toward himself has a direct bearing on how he lives all parts of his life. In fact, self-esteem is the mainspring that slates each of us for success or failure as a human being".

Dorothy Corkille Briggs
Your Child's Self-Esteem.

A. Levels of Self-Esteem

Each person who reads this book has a particular level of self-worth. Levels can be usefully categorised into high, middle and low self-esteem.

HIGH SELF-ESTEEM:

- Independent
- Open and spontaneous
- Optimistic, excited and challenged by life
- Flexible
- Direct and clear communicator
- Owns own problems, feelings, perceptions, ambitions etc.
- Emotional closeness with a few significant others
- Acceptance of self and others
- Respects and values others' differences
- Listens
- Can take criticism and feedback
- Tolerant of frustration
- Physically healthy
- Emotionally mature
- Encouraging of self and others
- Realistic awareness of strengths and weaknesses
- Sees weaknesses as opportunities for strength
- Problem-solver
- Expressive of all feelings
- Resistance to conformity
- Seeks support, advice, help, comfort when needed
- Whole-hearted involvement in all aspects of life
- Trusts and values self
- Caring of others
- Positively firm with self and others who attempt to impose artificial values upon him/her
- Cares for environment
- Spiritual
- Needs privacy

MIDDLE SELF-ESTEEM:

- Dependent
- Approval seeker
- People pleaser
- Difficulties in seeking support, help, advice etc.
- Cautious and unadventurous
- Fearful of 'new' situations
- Can take some criticism
- Moderate degree of optimism
- Critical of others' difference
- Threatened by opposition
- Expressive of some feelings
- Conformist
- Doubts about various aspects of self: physical, intellectual, social etc.
- Unsure
- General feeling of dissatisfaction
- Blaming of others
- Denial of problems
- Insecure in relationships
- Compares oneself to others
- Jealous of others' success, possessions etc.
- Critical of self and others
- Some neglect of physical welfare
- Aggressive or passive
- Intolerant of frustration
- Compliant or rigid
- Lives in the future
- Low autonomy
- Very ambitious
- Hostile sense of humour
- Perfectionist
- Tendencies to worry and anxiety

LOW SELF-ESTEEM:

- Highly dependent
- Pessimistic and fatalistic
- No sense of 'good' about self
- Condemning of self
- Extreme perfectionism
- 'Drop-out'
- Extreme fear of new situations
- Highly critical of all aspects of self
- Believes everybody else is better off
- Deep inferiority complex or a superiority complex (which is a cover-up of a sense of inferiority)
- Lonely and isolated
- Inability to form close and deep emotional relationships
- Sees oneself as unlovable
- Sometimes suicidal
- Rigid and inflexible
- Highly blaming of others or total denial of vulnerabilities
- Bottles up feelings or can be dangerously aggressive and violent
- Neglectful of physical welfare
- Rejecting of self
- Possessive of others
- Constant need for reassurance
- Manipulative of others
- Feelings easily hurt
- Highly sensitive to criticism
- Engages in distorted communication (eg. hostile silences, sulking, sarcasm, cynicism, blaming, ridiculing).
- Resistant to change
- Cannot take compliments or positive feedback
- Continuously unhappy
- Troubled relationships with others

- Worrier
- Highly prone to anxiety and depression
- Moody
- Feels different from all others
- Guilty about pleasure experiences for self
- Fears rejection
- Fearful of mistakes and failure
- Indecisive
- Lives life according to 'shoulds', 'should not's', 'have to's', 'musts' and 'ought to's'.
- Ashamed of self
- Feels life is not worth living
- Over-involvement or under-involvement in other people's lives
- Constantly trying to prove self

A teacher's level of self-esteem determines his/her level of professional esteem: high self-esteem leading to being an effective teacher and middle/low self-esteem leading to levels of ineffectiveness.

B. Origins of Self-Esteem

The causes of self-esteem lie principally in the early experiences of childhood. These early relationships with the significant adults in our lives (parents, relatives, teachers) were generally of a mixed nature in terms of being positive and negative. The positive interactions formed an image of being lovable and capable, whilst the negative ones developed a sense of unlovability and incapability. Clearly, the emphasis which obtained determines the level of self-esteem. Parents, teachers, and others are mirrors for children: the child who mostly experiences physical and emotional affection, affirmation, praise, encouragement, support, tenderness, listening, challenge, play, positive firmness etc. forms a healthy self-image whilst the child who frequently experiences absence of affection, or caring that is unfeeling, ridiculing, scolding, critical, physically abusive and who endures hostile silences, unrealistic demands and standards, negative labelling etc. develops an inferior image of self. No child has all completely positive experiences and as a result there are very few people with high self-esteem. Most people have middle self-esteem and a sizeable number have low levels.

One of the major sources of neuroses in our society and which few escape being influenced by is **conditionality**. A conditional upbringing breeds anxiety, uncertainty and insecurity and its intensity determines levels of anxiety and dependency. Conditional valuing means that one is loved, not for one's person or being, but for one's behaviour. Love then becomes a weapon to be used when children do not measure up to behavioural expectations. It reminds me of a young mother whose parents had both been teachers and highly demanding in terms of 'being perfect'. This young woman had a young child of less than two years in age. The child was always dressed 'to the nines', perfect. Inevitably, one day the child messed her perfect little suit. If she did mother lost control and began to shout at the child: "Mother doesn't love you anymore, she doesn't love you - she doesn't love you" - and she kept at it and at it. The child went very quiet and was as 'good as gold' for the rest of the day. An hour after being put to bed that night there were cries and roars from the child's room. Mother ran upstairs and into the bedroom to find the child standing up in her cot convulsed with crying. On seeing her mother the child immediately blubbered: "Mummy, Mummy, do you love me". The child clearly had had a nightmare awakening her to the unresolved trauma of that day. How clever of the child's psyche! The message to the mother was "If you keep withdrawing love from me because of my behaviour my life will become a nightmare". Children's nightmares are often messages to parents, teachers and other adults about conflicts inside the child regarding relationships with adults.

Conditions for love operate within most family and educational systems. Typical conditions are:

Be Good

Be Perfect

Be Like Me

Be Quiet

Be Clever
Be Successful
Be Kind
Be Funny
Be Pretty
Be Handsome
Be Irish
Be Unionist
Be Catholic
Be Busy
Be Like Your Brother/Sister

In the classroom it is known that teachers make more eye contact with, lean towards and ask questions of children whom they consider 'bright pupils'. Every child, indeed every adult, needs to shout from the rooftops, **"I am not my behaviour"**. Relationships are broken time and time again over bits of behaviour. It is always important to let others know what behaviours please and displease but only within the context of an enduring valuing relationship. Do not throw out the baby with the bath water.

The most common phobia of all is the fear of public speaking. A clear condition that was imposed on nearly everybody was 'not to make a fool of oneself' and hence public speaking becomes a threat to self-esteem. Research indicates that the children of teachers tend to be more psychologically at risk than the children of any other professional group. As a teacher, how could I have a fool of a child!

Cutting the ties that bind us and the conditions that enchain us, is one of the primary tasks of building self-esteem. Conditionality breeds all sorts of dependencies - on success, acceptance, approval, performance, physical appearance. The reverse side of the conditional coin is fear - fears of failure, rejection, criticism, loss of prestige, loss of physical looks. Fear in its turn creates negative, pessimistic, fatalistic and tentative attitudes and thoughts to various aspects of life and leads to behaviours that are either of an avoidant, shy, withdrawing or hidden nature or are aggressive, over-bearing, intense or blaming in style. The combination and intensity of all these emotions, attitudes and behaviours can have a profound effect on physical health.

C. Self-Esteem and Teaching

In the classroom the teacher with middle to low self-esteem tends to be defensive, sensitive to criticism, intolerant of difference from his/her view point and to personalise students' inappropriate behaviours as messages about his or her performance as a teacher rather than as a revelation of some inner conflict within the student. **Staying separate** from students' irresponsible behaviour is a key issue for teachers. However, a vulnerability to criticism blinds the teachers to this reality and unless this vulnerability is resolved it is difficult to stay separate. The vulnerable teacher also projects his or her own dependencies onto students, particularly those involving performance and success. In the case of personalisation the teacher confuses the students' troublesome behaviours with his own identity whereas with projection the teacher confuses his own behaviour with the student's identity.

An example of **personalisation** comes from the case of a fourteen year old student who was sent to me because he had been suspended from school. The suspension was a sanction for writing in the class workbook "fuck you teacher". On reading it the teacher reacted (personalised) and complained to her principal that 'nobody treats me like that' - the boy was duly suspended. Certainly the boy's written aggression was unacceptable but it was a statement, albeit hidden, about the boy not about the teacher. The boy needed to be educated to communicate in a more appropriate way. The hidden issue, which neither principal nor class teacher had looked for, was that the class teacher had seriously embarrassed the boy in front of his peers and on sitting down after the experience, feeling hugely angry, he wrote his aggressive statement. He later forgot about it, and later on in the day had handed up his workbook for evaluation. Both teacher and student could have learned much from this incident. As a teacher one does not have the right to embarrass students in front of their peers. Sarcasm, cynicism, ridicule and scoldings are unfair weapons to be used in classrooms. The use of them triggers defences against threats to self-esteem, such as aggressive behaviour. The class teacher in the case above could have benefitted from becoming aware of her unproductive action and also from apologising to the boy with a determination not to hurt him again. The boy, in his turn, could have been taught how to communicate his grievance clearly, directly and discreetly to the teacher and made aware that any form of aggression is unacceptable and deserves some sanction. Certainly, such an outcome would have strengthened the relationship between the student and the teacher.

Projection is present in the person who attempts to establish his worth through the behaviour or person of another. So, for example, the teacher who is dependent on others for approval, may put undue pressure on his or her students to academically perform so that (s)he can gain approval from colleagues, parents and students themselves. It is now well established that suicide increases around examination times, especially Leaving Certificate and First University Examinations. The suicidal student, feeling unable to meet the expectations (projections) of parents will commit suicide rather than facing the humiliation of failure and the consequent rejection by parents. A classic illustration of the devastating effects of projection (people living their lives through their children or students) was a case of two brothers I helped when I was practising in England. Both boys were taught by both of their parents in primary school (rarely a good idea !). The projection from both parents was that their sons should be top of the class. There was a two year gap in age between the boys. The older boy certainly failed to match the unrealistic expectations and was beaten, ridiculed, scolded, criticised, negatively labelled and frequently compared to his brother. It is well to be aware that **an act of comparison is an act of rejection**. It rejects the person who is being compared and puts pressure on the person to whom one is compared. The younger boy first came to my attention when he was 16 years of age. He had already been labelled schizophrenic. During conversations with him I would notice his attention had wandered and I would ask "Where are you now?", "Oh, I'm a Maths Teacher in the best school in England and the A-level results just came out and my class has got the highest results in the whole of England". This sad young man had hundreds of fantasies and lived ninety per cent of the time in a fantasy world. He had begun this retreat into an imaginary world at five years of age. To label him 'schizophrenic' did not help as once again he experienced 'not being good enough'. His delusional world was a strategy to protect him from a very painful reality of parental rejection - hardly insanity!! A relevant question here is if one lives up to the condition for love does one achieve a fulfilling life? Not so, because one is always anxious about not measuring up. The life of the brother of the boy being discussed brings home this latter point. He went on to do excellent A-levels and the following October went to University. At the end of his first University year he failed two components of his examinations. This was his first experience of academic failure and he knew well what the consequences would be when the news was brought home. What was he to do? Suicide was a high probability. Fortunately, he did not choose that path. However, he did not repeat the examinations in the Autumn for two reasons, one, he was afraid he might fail again, and , two, he was terrified that it would be discovered by his parents that he had failed already. The beginning of October came and a horrifying dilemma faced him. Keeping his secret he packed his bags and pretended he was heading back to University. For two years he lived alone in a bedsitter in Birmingham until he finally 'broke down' under the strain of the pretence and fear of the consequences of discovery. Like his brother I met him in the admission ward of a psychiatric hospital.

D. Self-Esteem and Teacher Training

The above is not meant as criticism of teachers. Indeed, the training programmes for teachers of both primary and secondary education leave a lot to be desired. All teachers know of the three R's, but what about the three I's: Initiation, Induction and In-service. Our **initiation** into teaching certainly provided us with a reasonable grounding on **What** to teach. However, the **How** to teach was badly neglected. The **How** entails understanding the emotional, social, sexual, spiritual, physical, sensual and creative modes of human behaviour. It also includes knowledge of the effects of conflict on children both in the home and school and means of resolving conflict. A knowledge of communication processes is essential, particularly those processes that aid the development of self-esteem of students. The areas of staff-development, staff cohesiveness and co-operation, stress management, whole school approaches, leadership, conflict resolution within staffs and basic counselling skills need also to be included in teacher training. The three main sources of stress in an increasingly pressurised teaching profession are role demands, difficult students and staff relationships. In my experience the latter is the greatest source of stress - this is true of many other professions as well. Many school staffs are characterised by cliques, resentments, rivalry, open hostility, hidden resentments, teachers isolated in their classrooms, autocratic leadership, poor morale, lack of co-operation, devisiveness on key issues, poor affirmation, hostile silences etc. These non-supportive environments reflect and have a detrimental effect on the level of self-esteem of each staff member. More sadly, its shadow casts itself beyond the staffroom into the classrooms. Again, this is not to blame teachers but to highlight the lack of training and consequent poor insight into these matters.

If initiation into teaching leaves a lot to be desired, **induction** is a total non starter. My first experience of teaching in a second-level school was a major shock to my enthusiasm. The school was in North Dublin and dressed in a three piece grey suit with leather briefcase, I walked down the corridors of the school to the students' whistling of the James Bond theme. I met the vice-principal, was presented with my time-table and shown to my classroom. When I looked through the glass into the classroom the students were literally throwing chairs and desks at each other. I visibly paled. Apparently, car tyre slashing was another favourite student occupation. The school was a veritable jungle. Not surprisingly, staff turnover was very high. There was no way my training (B.A. and Higher Diploma in Education) equipped me to deal with these students' very obvious and deep social, emotional and behavioural problems. Most of the day went into attempts to control students.

I approached the principal for advice, support, back-up - plain and simple help. However, the response was that I was responsible for my own classes and any problems therein. I resigned after three weeks. I later found a job in the opposite type school - that of over-control. That too had its problems but at least one felt safe. When I completed my doctorate training in clinical psychology I was still and, indeed happily, obliged to do two years of supervision under a Senior Clinical Psychologist. A similar system is needed for young teachers. A two year induction time under the supervision of teachers with a minimum of five years experience would benefit the novice teacher. It also provides a formal recognition of the older teacher's experience. Principals of schools also need to be sensitive to the needs and vulnerabilities of younger teachers during this induction period and provide advice, support and affirmation.

The third 'I' is **in-service training**. All professions are in evolution and the need to stay abreast of developments in theory and practice is essential. Indeed, the process needs to be an integral part of a professional's life. Amazingly, this has not been the case within education. Certainly, many individual teachers, at their own expense, have pursued post-graduate courses but the Department of Education has only weakly endorsed but never financed or encouraged such development. Irish society has changed radically within the last twenty years. The rapid decline of religion, the massive rise in marital breakdown and separation, the increase in single-parent families, the influence of the media, the development of a more pluralist society, the unemployment crisis, changing values and morals, all of these changes influence what happens in schools. Twenty years ago discipline problems were a rare phenomenon in classrooms. At that time, children were members of three main systems: the family, the school and the church. Authoritarianism ruled the day and was predictably and consistently applied and reinforced across the three systems. Fear was the major weapon of control within the three systems. Whilst this approach was successful in effecting quiet it did not at all mean that learning was promoted. Evidence for the latter is the high level of adult literacy and numeracy problems in this country. Furthermore, authoritarianism fosters passivity or, for some brave souls who rebel, aggression. Neither of these reactions are healthy for mature development. Parents and teachers need to educate children for responsibility and self control - not control by others. A major stressor now within many schools is students with emotional, social and behavioural difficulties and consequent discipline problems. Matters are very confusing both for students and teachers. If, for example, a student comes from a democratic family system, which fosters self-control and responsibility, and he comes into a school which is authoritarian and fosters control by others, then the student will be confused and sometimes reactionary. Furthermore, within any one school, the student may experience a democratic system in one classroom and an authoritarian one in another. Similarly, if a student comes from an authoritarian family system into a democratic school or classroom system, confusion will also result. Until a situation of predictability and consistency is established across the main systems of which children are members, discipline problems are likely to persevere and even escalate. Children will no longer accept authoritarianism, and rightly so! A democratic system that values each child as a unique human being, that heralds the capability of the child, that is affirmative, supportive, caring, fair, just and is positively firm in the face of irresponsible behaviours must be developed within each major system. **Predictability** and **consistency** are hallmarks of any effective social system. Their importance underlies the developing awareness of the need for close liaison between homes and schools, of whole-school approaches that emphasise effective inter-staff communication, staff development and staff cohesiveness. No longer can a teacher be left isolated in the classroom to cope with the multiple emotional, behavioural, educational, sexual, social and spiritual problems of students. In-service training then needs to primarily focus on a greater psychological and sociological understanding of student and teacher behaviour, of effective responses to emotional, behavioural and social problems in students and professional colleagues, on staff development in terms of effective communication systems, stress management, cohesiveness, problem-solving and more positive approaches to teaching. In-service courses also need to focus on leadership style, management systems and personal development.

E. Changing Self-Esteem

There are two interdependent factors in personal change: **awareness** and **action**. Awareness of itself is not sufficient. Having identified your level of self-esteem, the conditions that you believe make for acceptance by others and self, the use of introjecting and projecting styles of communication, you are now ready for change through the use of counter-conditioning covert and overt behaviours.

The principle awareness is that behaviour does not determine my worth as a human being; behaviour is my means of experiencing this world and neither adds nor detracts from my unique humanity. In the same vein, all behaviour has a function and failure and mistakes are means to further learning and growth and are not statements about capability. Furthermore, any act of comparison of myself with others is an act of rejection of self.

To change self-esteem entails using the same means that brought about your present level of value of self. As has been seen, it is the relationships you experienced with parents, teachers and other significant adults during your childhood that principally define your self-esteem. If the cause then of middle or poor self-esteem is relationships then the 'cure' must also be a relationship. However, it is not your relationship with others as an adult that will raise self-esteem. Many adults continue to try to achieve security through their relationships with others but this is dependency and can lead to all types of problems in relationships (possessiveness, controlling, criticism, manipulation) to conflict and a further blow to self-esteem. The major way to change your self-esteem is by means of a relationship with self. This relationship must have all the characteristics that a loving and affirmative parent would have towards his or her child. It needs to be primarily **emotional** in nature so that all your thoughts and actions are infused with a valuing and celebration of self. Valuing and celebration must be an every moment experience in your daily life so that the flood of affirming actions sweeps out the old tide of rejection of self, conditionality, negative thinking, avoidance of challenge, aggression or passivity, and neglect of physical well-being. Change occurs by ensuring that all actions are of a self-valuing and self-caring nature, whether they have to do with rest, hygiene, driving, career, diet, relationships, physical exercise, life-style, school discipline, and so on. To rush and race, eat unhealthy foods, miss meals, rush meals, criticise oneself, compare oneself with others, be aggressive, accept aggression from others, be passive in the face of others, be manipulative, irresponsible, possessive or controlling in actions, overwork regularly, over-indulge frequently in any food or beverage, never say 'No' to others, people-please at all times, look for approval from others - these are all examples of lack of value of self. Reverse the cycle: do everything calmly and in a relaxed manner, eat foods that nurture you, give yourself adequate time to eat and digest, listen to self, encourage yourself to do your best, see mistakes and failures as opportunities for learning, be assertive about your own views whilst respecting others, be spontaneous and open, non-conformist, honest, unaccepting of any artificial goals that people may attempt to impose on you, be responsive to your own needs and to the reasonable needs of others, be moderate in your intake of food and beverages, be regular in physical exercise and balanced in your life-style in terms of allocating time to meeting your various needs. Balanced life-style is a good indicator of high self-esteem. It entails being responsive to all your needs, emotional, social, sexual, physical, behavioural (skills development), cognitive, spiritual, recreational and occupational. Another indicator of high self-esteem is being calm and relaxed, undefensive in the face of others' problematic behaviours. Changing your concept of self is an endless process that needs to be consistently worked on at all times. The old rejecting and dependency ways are strongly ingrained and it is only through constant reinforcement of an accepting cycle of behaviours that these old damaging ways will be eradicated. The rewards are high: security, independence, freedom to be your self, spontaneity, unconditionality with yourself and others, clear and direct in communication, peacefulness and tranquillity, openness to change, to others and to life and increased potential for self-fulfillment.

● *Checklist for Self-Esteem Enhancement*

To what degree (0-5) do you relate to yourself in terms of the following range of covert and overt behaviours?

- ❏ Affirmation
- ❏ Acceptance
- ❏ Praise
- ❏ Encouragement
- ❏ Understanding
- ❏ Compassion
- ❏ Listening
- ❏ Valuing
- ❏ Loving
- ❏ Humorous
- ❏ Challenging
- ❏ Relaxed
- ❏ Balanced life-style
- ❏ Positive self-talk
- ❏ Supportive
- ❏ Nurturance
- ❏ Healthy Diet
- ❏ Regular Exercise
- ❏ Positive Firmness
- ❏ Responsible
- ❏ Kind
- ❏ Caring
- ❏ Fair
- ❏ Belief in one's capability
- ❏ Unconditionality

● Changing Communication Patterns

It has been pointed out already that a major give-away of self-esteem problems is the defensive communication patterns of **introjection** and **projection.** Introjection reveals identity confusion with other's opinions or feedback and projection also indicates identity problems and the passing of the responsibility for your happiness and fulfillment in life onto others. When you introject or personalise, others will perceive you as being hypersensitive, easily hurt and vulnerable and as somebody in need of protection. When you project, others will see you as dominating, aggressive, pushy or manipulative, passive, needy, dependent or passively-aggressive. Both types of communication inevitably lead to conflict and further exacerbation of low levels of self-esteem.

Introjection and Projection

Personalisation or introjection of others' behaviours arise from dependency on people for acceptance and approval with consequent fears of rejection, disapproval, criticism and failure. Dependency in turn arises from poor acceptance and valuing of self (middle/low self-esteem) which in turn arises from unresolved conflicts in childhood when either conditional parenting/teaching or total neglect left one feeling highly vulnerable. It is good to see this process clearly as reducing or overcoming personalisation is only possible when all the aspects that have contributed to its development are perceived and worked upon.

It can be seen from the illustration below that communication patterns are but the crest of the wave of an underlying sea of emotional experiences. Clearly, the more you correct your relationship with yourself (parenting self) so that you are unconditionally accepting of self the more that each level of the problem hierarchy will become resolved. The more you elevate your self-esteem the more you reduce dependency on others, extinguish fears and become separate from parents and others. When that happens, communication patterns will automatically change. However, the process of self-change is a long one and in the meantime it is useful to

Introjection / Projection
↕
Fears of Rejection
Failure, criticism ....
↕
Dependency on Others
for acceptance/approval
↕
Middle/Poor Self-Esteem
(poor acceptance/valuing of self)
↕
Unresolved Childhood Conflicts
*(due either to conditional parenting/teaching
or total parental neglect)*

become more aware of destructive styles of communication and to replace them with more constructive methods.

Like any other process of change, awareness and action are the key elements. The recognition of the tendency to personalise other people's behaviours as saying something about self is the first step to changing that misinterpretation. The second step is the awareness that no matter what another person says or does it is a statement about that person . The first covert action step to take when, for example, a person sends you 'a you message', like 'you're insensitive', is to ask yourself quickly "what is this saying about the person addressing me" and then return the message to them in order to get to the hidden "I" message. In the present example the best way to return the "you message" is to say "in what way do you find me insensitive". The answer might be another "you" message, like "you're never here for me" or "you're always out" or "you never listen". So, once again you bat back the message by saying - taking the examples given - "in what way do you need me here for you", or "do you want me home more often" or "what am I not hearing from you?" Communication has stayed open and the "I" messages will now begin to emerge, such as "I am lonely and need more contact with you" or "I need to go out socially with you" or "I need for you to hear my opinions and needs". What is clear now is that the original "you" messages (projections by the other person) hid "I" messages about blocked needs. If you had personalised these messages and had either withdrawn or attacked back, then communication would have broken down, the relationship would suffer and both persons would go away hurt and bruised and the blocked needs would remain unmet. At least when needs are expressed there is now opportunity to explore whether or not you are in a position to meet the needs. If the needs are reasonable then a 'yes' is, generally, in order, if unreasonable, then a 'no' is in order; if somewhat difficult to meet then negotiation is necessary. What is important is that all the time you have held onto your own value in yourself and have stayed separate but caring in your response to the other person's communication. The steps then to reducing introjection are:

1. Awareness of tendency to personalise
2. Awareness that verbal and non-verbal communication are one hundred per cent about the person addressing you.
3. Covert action: "what's this saying about the person sending the message".
4. Return message to sender in order to discover hidden "I" message.
5. Hold onto your value of self.
6. Respond appropriately to revealed blocked needs.
7. Affirm your need to keep communication open at all times.

As has been outlined above **projection** is only the tip of the iceberg when it comes to understanding human vulnerability. Nonetheless, as with introjection, it is necessary to take charge and change this destructive means of relating to others. The initial steps are similar to those for changing personalisation: awareness of tendency to project and awareness that all behaviour coming from you is about you and that others are not responsible for you. The first covert action is **owning** all aspects of self. Below is a variation of Virginia Satir's Declaration of Self-Esteem which highlights the absolute need of adults to own everything about themselves.

DECLARATION OF MY UNIQUENESS

I wonder at my unique being.

I am a once off happening in this universe that will never reoccur.

I love, value, celebrate and own everthing about me.

I love and care for my body which carries every aspect of me. I will nurture, exercise, rest and accept every aspect of my body. I do not want my body to be like anybody else's.

I love, value, and wonder at the limitless capacity of my mind.

I own my mistakes and failures and realise these do not in any way take away from my wondrous capacity. I see mistakes and failures purely as opportuities for further learning.

I enjoy my achievements and successes but do not hold onto any of them as indicators of my worth. My worth and value are independent of all my actions.

I strongly distinguish between my being and my behaviour.

I am unconditional in my regard for myself and others.

No action on the part of myself or others takes away from my worth, value and uniqueness.

I own and take responsibility for all my thoughts, images ambitions, words and actions, whether they be of a positive or negative nature and whether they be towards others or myself.

There are many things I have done or may do that I regret or will regret but I am determined to grow from these experiences and learn to love myself and others more deeply every day.

I will be honest and open about behaviour that is distressful to me but in a way that does not put the other person down.

Equally, I will be open and listen to what others have to say to me about what behaviours of mine they find distressful and I will take responsibility for any neglect or hurt I may have caused.

No matter what happens I will not cease to care for myself or others.

I know I have immense abilities to grow and develop in this world. I can touch, see, feel, hear, think, imagine, say and do. I can be deeply close to others. I can be productive. I can make sense and meaning of what often seems an uncaring and cruel world.

I will always remain true to my uniqueness and not allow others to impose artificial goals upon me.

I am unique, perfect in my being and once I remain in possession of my wondrous being, I can create a better world for me and others.

When I project I put the responsibility for my life onto another. For example, if I say, "you make me miserable", or "you never consult me", or "you never consider me" I am giving you a lot of power over me and I am abrogating my own responsibility for my own needs. In communicating with you, having owned my own needs, I want to now send you an "I" message about some need I have. Taking the examples above, I might say: "when I'm left alone every evening I feel miserable and lonely and I would like more time with you" or " I would like to be consulted on issues related to my work in this school" or "I would like my needs to develop my career to be considered". Having expressed your need, the next step is to accept that **your message is not a command** but a request and therefore you allow the other person the right to say 'yes' or 'no' to your need without either response affecting your value and respect for the other person or for yourself. Remember that you **own** your own needs and meeting those needs is your responsibility. The steps to overcoming projection can be outlined as follows:

1. Recognition of tendency to use projection as a means of getting your needs in life met.
2. Awareness that projection is a mirror of your dependency on others.
3. Own everything about yourself.
4. Send an "I" message regarding an unmet need.
5. Allow the receiver the freedom to say 'yes' or 'no' to an expressed need (whether reasonable, unreasonable or difficult).
6. Take responsibility for getting your own need met.

A good question is what do you do when reasonable needs - for example, for students to be responsible and orderly in class, or for a principal to support you in classroom management issues, or for a partner to respond to your sexual needs - are consistently not being met? You must hold onto the realisation that you cannot force another (whether through aggression, manipulation, withdrawal) to meet your needs. Unfortunately, the reverse often happens and accounts for much conflict within relationships, staffrooms and classrooms. The first step is to enquire from the person concerned (whether student, principal or partner in the examples given) what is it that blocks him/her from meeting what you believe is a reasonable need. In actively listening to his/her response you might discover that the person has some deeper, even more expedient need than yours, that is not being met. Again, taking the examples above, you might find that your principal lacks confidence, is threatened by failure and has an unmet need for acceptance from staff members or the student who is uncooperative has a massive unmet need to be valued by others or that your partner, who is not responsive to your sexual needs, has an unmet emotional need for you be affectionate at other times than just in bed. In responding to the unmet need of the other person what often happens is that the person then becomes more disposed towards meeting your needs. By staying open to the other person, inspite of him/her not meeting your need, you have now facilitated positive movement and growth in the relationship where hidden needs are revealed and, when reasonable, met. Sometimes it will arise that the other person is seriously blocked within themselves and in spite of your repeated attempts to discover the blocked needs, the person remains closed off to your understanding and to your needs. Such a person needs professional help to move out of their sub-consciously 'stuck' position. The important point to bear in mind is that their being blind to your worth is a message about them **not** about you.

When you begin to work on being more positive and independent in your communication with others, at the beginning you may fail more often than succeed, as old patterns, like old soldiers, die hard. Persist and the gains will be a more valuing relationship with yourself and others.

2. KEY ISSUES

The foregoing has highlighted some key issues and principles for teachers primarily in the area of self-esteem and professional development .

- Personal and professional effectiveness are strongly related to one's level of self-esteem.

- The causes of self-esteem lie principally in the early experiences of childhood within the home and school.

- In teacher training, the 'how' to teach needs as much emphasis as the 'what' to teach.

- Continual updating of theory and practice must be an integral part of a teacher's career.

- Person and behaviour are separate issues.

- Conditionality breeds neuroses and, in extreme cases, psychoses.

- Staying separate is the key to effective relationships.

- Personalisation (introjection) is a misinterpretation of another person's behaviour as saying something about oneself and leads to conflict and breakdown of communication.

- Projection involves transferring responsibility for one's own needs onto others and leads to blaming, criticism, coercion or withdrawal, hostility, resentment, sullen silences and, ultimately, to conflict and communication breakdown.

- Both personalisation and projection are indicators of dependency on others and middle or poor self-esteem.

3. KEY TASKS

- There are two interdependent factors in personal change: awareness and action.

- Identify your own level of self-esteem.

- Identify and free yourself of the conditions you set for acceptance and value of yourself by self and others.

- Recognise and correct your use of introjecting and projecting styles of distorted communication.

- Ensure that all your actions are of a self-valuing and self-caring nature.

- Unconditionally accept and value yourself.

CHAPTER THREE

The Staffroom

1. STAFF RELATIONSHIPS

2. COMMUNICATION AND STAFF RELATIONSHIPS

    A. Open/Relating Communication

    B. Defensive Communication

- *Judgemental*
- *Controlling*
- *Strategic*
- *Neutral*
- *Superior*
- *Certain*

    C. Expression of Needs

3. SEEKING AND RECEIVING STAFF SUPPORT

    A. 'Weakness' is Strength

    B. Welfare and Emergency Feelings

    C. Dependency Versus Independence

4. STAFF MORALE

    A. Staff Interactions

1. STAFF RELATIONSHIPS

One of my experiences of working in many schools over the last eight years is that staff relationships are rarely of a healthy, open, cooperative and dynamic nature. The contrary is often the case: rivalry, hostility, cliques, gossip, resentment, isolation, fear, aggression, dependency, criticism and alienation. Research, as has been already pointed out, has isolated staff relationships as a major contributor to stress in teaching. This is not good for a profession that so needs the back-up of colleagues to deal with the rising tide of stressors within teaching. However, teaching as a profession is quite defensive and slow to be influenced by either progressive people within the profession or professionals outside the profession. One reason for this is that many teachers' identities are tied up sub-consciously with their professional performance and any feedback or suggestions for change are read as threats to self-esteem thereby giving rise to defensive behaviours of denial, non-cooperation, non-listening or hostility. It is of interest to all members of staff when a colleague has a self-esteem problem as the manifestations of it are likely to affect all relationships and activities within the school. The teacher with low self-esteem may be the passive, quiet teacher who works extremely hard, putting immense pressure on herself or himself and, very often on students, but makes no demands of his or her colleagues. Frequently this teacher may have control difficulties within the classroom. However, (s)he does not seek help from colleagues and the problems continue to escalate. On the other hand, a teacher with low self-esteem may also manifest inner conflicts through an over-bearing, aggressive manner. This teacher may use authoritarian control methods and can sometimes be both verbally and physically violent. At staff-meetings (s)he may be uncooperative, dominating and abusive of anyone who does not see things his or her way. All these maladaptive behaviours are a screen to a very great underlying insecurity. The dominant, aggressive teacher tries to get approval and acceptance by compelling these responses from others. The passive, unassertive teacher gains approval by being the 'people pleaser' always trying to meet the needs of others.

Both of these teachers, who actually have a similar underlying problem of self-esteem, make for a difficult staff environment as both are highly sensitive to feedback and resistant to changes. Nonetheless, it is important that all staff be concerned to develop mature relationships, and, particularly, to create a supportive and positive environment so that colleagues with self-esteem difficulties (which we all have to some degree) may find the safety to express their needs and concerns and get the help they need to resolve their inner conflicts. One of the primary means of establishing positive staff relationships is mature communication.

2. COMMUNICATION AND STAFF RELATIONSHIPS

The type of communication that is most used in many staff rooms, not just school staff rooms, is of a nature that creates relationship problems and damages self-esteem of members of that staff. It can be an eye-opener to check how rarely you use open/relating communication patterns and how often you use distorted communication patterns; all of which lead to an unsupportive and threatening environment.

A. Open/Relating Communication

There are two major patterns of communication: open or relating and defensive. The former, a rare phenomenon, is essential for the fulfillment of individual and staff goals. It is a style of communication wherein each is aware of and experiences openess, closeness and understanding of the other and what is discussed is pertinent, relevant and appropriate. For teachers to engage in this type of relating you need to have - yes, that same old factor comes up once again - high self-esteem, a feeling of adequacy, competency and trust in your ability to assist another. The teacher also needs to be aware of weaknesses and vulnerabilities and be able to reveal them when expedient. The latter can only occur within a supportive staff environment.

B. Defensive Communication

The more common form of relating is defensive and this takes many forms. Defensive patterns of communication are inefficient and twisted and produce a circular reaction of defensiveness. When you examine the list below you may be surprised how often you use these forms of interacting even though they seriously weaken the self-esteem of both communicator and receiver and the relationship between them.

Defensive Communication Patterns

● *Judgemental*

When a teacher is judgemental (s)he accuses and criticises which results in a defensive response from the other person of either withdrawal or a criticism in return.
Examples are

- criticising, name calling, characterising, blaming (eg. "You're a fool", "You never listen", "You're a typical teacher").
- cross-examining, interrogating, fact-finding, (eg. "Are you sure you know what you're talking about?", "Are you telling me the truth?").
- praising and approving (eg. "You're a great teacher", "You prepared a good agenda for the meeting", "That's a brilliant piece of work").

Many people have difficulty in grasping that praising and approving can have negative effects on relationships and on self-esteem. When these messages are sent they are generally well intended (unless there is a hidden agenda, then they are manipulative) but when they are phrased as in the examples above they imply that the sender can judge the other's performance. Such messages also raise the possibility that the next performance may be disapproved of, perhaps only by failure to show approval. The relationship created is that of judge/supplicant. Does that mean you should never praise or approve others' performances? Certainly not, but there are two issues to be considered here - one, it is always better to put the emphasis on effort rather than performance, as every effort is an attainment. The second issue is that when praise or approval is expressed in a judgemental way - "you're a great lad" - it expresses nothing about the sender and therefore it is now a distorted message. Recall that all communications are about the sender. Therefore, it is far more accurate when communicating that you are impressed by (for example) a person's work or dress or grasp of a subject to say "I am impressed by your essay" or "I like the colours you are wearing" or "I am in awe of your grasp of this subject". The "I" message communicates something about your perception but allows the other to evaluate his or her own performance. Indeed, it is often wise when you wish to communicate your perception of another's behaviour that you first ask them how they see it.

● *Controlling*

When a teacher is controlling (s)he is authoritarian, threatening and moralistic; all of which produce reactions of either fright or fight, certainly defensiveness and either acquiesence or resistance and always resentment. The teacher who is controlling does not listen to the other's opinions or views and discounts that person's feelings. Depending on the reaction of the receiver these types of communication can either produce aggression or passivity, rebelliousness or control by others, fearfulness or authoritarianism. Controlling others implicitly communicates that the receiver is unable to be responsible for himself or herself and is in need of a controller, who, of course, is attempting to boost, in vain, his or her own self-esteem at the expense of another. It therefore damages the self-esteem of the receiver, creates defensiveness in the relationship and does nothing for the self-development of the sender.

Examples are:
- Directing, commanding, ordering (eg. "Do what you're told", "Get down to your work", "You must change...")
- Warning, threatening, punishing (eg. "If you bring up that I'll never talk to you again", "You'd better do what I say ....").

- Moralising, preaching ("Good people don't support divorce", "Do you know what you should do with your life.....", "Teachers should be able to control their classes .... ").

● *Strategic*

In this type of defensive communication the sender has hidden motivations - better known as 'hidden agendas' - and is strategically attempting to manipulate the other into meeting some hidden needs. It is akin to emotional blackmail except that it is happening at a covert level. If the receiver responds to the manipulation (s)he will be heartily reinforced but if (s)he refuses to cooperate, then outright rejection can speedily occur. It is clear that the person who engages in manipulation has a low level of self-esteem, otherwise (s)he would be open about needs and willing to accept whatever response the receiver would give. The strategy is to reduce risk so that failure is minimised and no humiliation experienced. However, this approach undermines the relationship between the two people as no openness, trust or genuineness are shown and it also weakens the self-esteem of the other as the sender's capacity to value, understand and responsibly respond to the other is not acted upon.

Examples are:
- Non-verbal manipulation: sulking, withdrawing, hostile silences, sighing.
- Verbal manipulation: "If you do that for me, I'll look after you", "Nobody sees how hard I have to work here".

● *Neutral*

When a teacher is neutral in communicating (s)he shows little or no concern or feeling for the other person. Somehow the teacher is threatened by either emotional closeness or emotional conflict and neutrality protects against venturing into affective areas or ways of relating that threaten self-esteem. Very often the teacher manifests 'the being busy syndrome' to protect himself or herself against rejection. Unfortunately, because others do not read the sender's neutrality as a protective device they can feel hurt, dismissed, unwanted and of little value. Once again the self-esteem of both parties and the relationship between them are weakened.

Examples are:
- Withdrawing, diverting (eg. "I won't discuss it any further", "That is the end of the matter").
- Ignoring, dismissing, responding 'on the run' (eg. "Don't be bothering me with that", "Can't stop now, must run...").
- Reassuring, excusing, consoling, sympathising (eg. "Time cures everything", " I'm sure he's not saying what you think he's saying").
- Me too messages (eg. "Didn't I have that trouble too", "Don't I know exactly how you feel").

● *Superior*

Basically the message being sent here is that "I know best" or "I am right" and "if you follow my advice you won't go wrong". The person who communicates in this superior way is, in reality, masking an inferiority complex. The need to be superior is an attempt to gain acceptance and approval from others. In reality it has the opposite effect as superiority deprives the receiver of the esteem-building experience of solving his or her own problems. It also encourages dependency in the receiver (which the sender needs in order to feel good) and it very often leads to conflict (eg. the receiver responds "Don't tell me how to lead my life"). A very wise rule of thumb is "never to give advice to an adolescent or adult unless they request it".

Examples are:
- Advising, recommending (eg. "What you should do is ....", "Why don't you leave teaching").
- Diagnosing, psychoanalysing (eg. "You're only saying that because you're tired", "You just don't like men, do you?", "It's just your period time").

● *Certain*

The certain type of communication is common in teachers who possess very rigid attitudes andwho tend to live their lives according to 'shoulds', 'should nots', 'musts' and 'ought to's'. (Rigidity is discussed in more detail in section 6 of this chapter). The need to be dogmatic and certain is again a means to gain acceptance and approval. To reveal any uncertainty and provisionalism in this teacher's eyes would be to show vulnerability and weakness and to risk disapproval. This type of communication does not value the other person's differences from the sender; indeed it emphasises the receiver's 'wrongness', invalidates his or her feelings and leads to defensiveness and lack of openness.

Example:
- Persuading, lecturing, arguing (eg. "I am absolutely right about this", "The fact is ....", "There is only one way to do this").

Defensive communication patterns are reflective of non-supportive environments, wherein the self-esteem of staff members' is frequently threatened, leading to lack of openness and trust and poor staff relationships.

Open communication is exactly the opposite of defensive communication:

Defensive Communication	*Open Communication*
Judgemental	Non-Judgemental
Controlling	Permissive
Strategic	Spontaneous
Neutral	Empathic
Superior	Equal
Certain	Provisional

It is encumbent on all staff members to practise communication patterns that create positive, open, caring, and trusting relationships, not only within the staffroom but also within the classroom as children tend to imitate the communication behaviours of significant adults in their life. Good staff morale makes it easier to establish a supportive staff environment. The real key to healthy staff relationships is where each member works to establish a high level of self-esteem within himself or herself.

C. Expression of Needs

Communication is principally about needs: when it is defensive people's needs are rarely met; when it is open needs are generally well met.

There are, in effect, four ways you can express a need. One way is to be **direct and clear**. For example, your principal has made a decision about your work and has not consulted you about it. You feel angry as you have a need to be consulted on matters affecting your responsibilities. You want to send a direct and clear message to John the school principal: "John, (direct) when decisions are made about my work without consultation with me, I feel angry and I'm asking that in future I be consulted on such matters". This kind of message is a rare phenomenon. What is more likely is that one of the following kinds of message is sent:

Indirect and clear

Direct and unclear

Indirect and unclear

Taking the example above, and using the indirect and clear mode, the message now becomes: "People (indirect) who make decisions about other people's work make me angry". John, the principal, can totally ignore this message as it is not addressed to him and he has no responsibility for deciphering your twisted messages. It is your responsibility to send a direct and clear message. The most typical way we communicate is in the **direct but unclear** mode so that the message to John now becomes: "John, you think you can do what you like in this school". Now the message is certainly directed to John - indeed there is a surfeit of 'you's' - but the content is totally masked. John has no clue what your outburst is all about. Regrettably, we are all masters of the 'you' message which says nothing at all about the sender of the message and thus the real message lies hidden. In an earlier section it was noted that messages are one hundred per cent about the sender. A 'you' message is then twisted and leads to either attack or flight on the part of the receiver. A typical defensive retort to the direct but unclear message in the example above is: "You're always complaining about something". Communication has now broken down as both parties are engaging in problematic communication patterns. The final type of communication, **indirect and unclear**, is totally distorted and leads to all types of relationship problems. Cynicism and sarcasm are examples of this pattern. In the present example the message becomes: "People can be so full of you know what".

The only healthy way to communicate is to use the direct and clear statement and make sure that the message is an "I" and not a 'you' message. 'You' messages are judgemental, critical, superior, certain, and they damage self-esteem. 'I' messages, on the other hand, are a total **owning** of one's own needs or perceptions and put no pressure on the other party to respond. As a result, the likelihood of communication remaining open is greater and all the time the communicator is respecting and valuing his or her colleague and is accepting the colleague's right to be different in outlook, philosophy and attitudes and allows his or her colleague the freedom to respond or not to respond.

Practice of direct and clear communication creates a supportive staffroom environment.

3. SEEKING AND RECEIVING STAFF SUPPORT

There are factors other than communication that also contribute to the development of a healthy staffroom climate. One factor is the seeking and receiving of help and support from one another. Again this behaviour is not common but when you look at the three requirements that need to be present for teachers to go to one another for support, you will understand what blocks the development of such mature consultation. The three requirements are:

A.   An understanding that seeking and receiving support is a necessary strength required for reducing stress and that this needs to become part of the daily working routine.

B.   An ability to value and respect your own feelings, to be able to identify them and to talk them through in full openness.

C.   An ability to be vulnerable, to trust and to receive the time, attention and care of another person.

A. 'Weakness' is Strength

The first requirement runs counter to what most of us learned: do not show weakness or vulnerability and do not ask for help. Indeed, many see asking for help as a weakness. The problem is that every time you suppress the need for support and help you miss the chance to grow. St. Paul said it very well: "When I am weak, I am strong". It is through accepting your weaknesses that you can grow in strength and knowledge and ability to cope. In any staff situation there is much expertise, wisdom, support, understanding and counsel available but it is seldom utilised. A young teacher can gain much from an older teacher. A teacher having problems with a particular class can get advice from a teacher who is having no problems with that class - clearly, what the latter is doing works and what the former is doing does not. Likewise, all teachers can gain from a sharing and a pooling of resources to deal with the most problematic students. The teacher left isolated with such students is unlikely to be successful. Many teachers are fearful of going to colleagues for help as they think that their colleagues will feel they should not be teaching if they are not able to cope. Unfortunately, in some cases their fears are not without ground. The safety of not being judged nor criticised is so important if teachers are to be able to go to each other for help. Nevertheless, you need to be able to get to a place of independence of the responses of colleagues and to be determined to grow from every vulnerability and weakness that arises.

B. Welfare and Emergency Feelings

The second requirement is concerned with expression of feelings which are the kernel issue of any communication. The difficulty is that most people do not value their feelings, particularly feelings like fear, anger, sadness, resentment, jealousy, guilt and so on. They see these latter feelings as 'bad' or 'negative'. Feelings like love, comfort, joy, confidence, enthusiasm are seen as 'good' or 'positive'. If you view certain feelings as negative then expression of them is difficult because of your own negative attitude and the threat of other people also seeing them in the same negative way. Even with the so called 'positive' feelings many people have difficulty in expressing them as they fear rejection. Men, in particular, are not good at expressing the 'good' feelings as stereotyping in childhood led to the inhibition of such feelings. Stereotyping has been kinder to women as generally they are much better at the expression of all feelings, except anger. As a result women tend to be physically healthier than men and outlive men by an average of eight years. Research has shown that men who over a long period of time persistently suppress or repress their feelings of grief, sadness, resentment, fear, threat and so on. are very prone to cardiovascular disease. Recent research indicates that women, who for background reasons other than stereotyping, 'bottle-up' feelings such as anger, loneliness, fear are prone to breast cancer. Inability to express hostility is also strongly associated with certain cancers.

It is important to emphasise the message that: "There are no such things as 'negative' or 'bad' feelings". As you will see **all feelings are positive** rather than positive/negative. I prefer to use the terms **Welfare** and **Emergency Feelings,** the former referring to the so-called 'good' feelings and the latter to the misnamed 'negative' feelings. Welfare feelings are well named as they indicate that you are presently in a 'welfare state' or you are experiencing a state of well being. On the other hand, emergency feelings are even more aptly labelled as they indicate that you are in an 'emergency' state and some action either covert or overt is needed to return you to a state of well being. Emergency feelings like fear and anger alert you to the need for emotional healing in the same way that physical pain alerts you to the need for physical healing. Both the emergency feeling and the physical pain are positive and necessary for the recognition of the need for action that will bring about a state of either emotional or physical well-being.

It is also wise to see that you cannot hurt yourself or others with feelings. For example, many people, particularly women, have difficulties in expressing anger. But anger is a feeling and it cannot hurt another person. However, actions hurt, whether verbal, non-verbal, written or physical. To express anger through aggression is abusive of another. But it is the action of aggression not the angry feeling that abuses the other. Anger is positive, it alerts you to some emergency situation and' it gives you the energy to act on that situation. When you feel anger exploding within you it is best to reduce its power to a manageable proportion before expressing it as otherwise it may express itself through aggression. Aggression, of its very nature, puts the other person down, breaks communication and leaves the issue unresolved. The best way to reduce built-up, unmanageable anger is through some type of physical activity. Also, in this situation it is always wise to remove yourself from the target (student, child, spouse, colleague, friend) of your anger. Remember your anger is a revelation about some unmet need of yours which needs to be expressed in an assertive, direct and clear way using an "I" message. It is not a message about the other person.

People rarely **own**, **respect** and **value** their feelings as expressions of unmet needs. The tendency of most of us is to suppress or to project emergency feelings either via aggression - "You're the one who makes me miserable" - or passive manipulation - "After all I have done for you and now you treat me in this way" - or the non-verbal manipulation of hostile silences, sulking etc. There is a far more serious sub-conscious response to feelings (either welfare or emergency) and that is **Repression**. The person who suppresses does not consciously realise that they are cutting off their feelings. Very often these people go around with a placid, smiling appearance - they do not seem to react to either expressions of welfare or emergency feelings from others and do not express these feelings themselves. An example comes from a teacher who came to me for help with an obsessive-compulsive problem of having to check and re-check regulators (light switches, taps, cooker switches) many times before going to bed at night or before leaving the house in the morning. Her main preoccupation was with taps, but the compulsion had generalised to other regulators.

The rationale that the teacher gave for her 'irrational' behaviours was that "I'm afraid of flooding the house". It took her hours to get to bed every night and frequently she would have to get out of the bed to re-check again. Similarly, in the mornings she rose early in order to be able to go through her checking rituals and often had to return home when half-way to school. She was in her early thirties and had had no heterosexual relationship to date. Neither did she have any close female friends. What eventually emerged was that she had enormous fear of the expression of any feelings whether of love or fear, anger, as these feelings were not expressed by her parents when she was a child. Neither could her parents receive any such feelings. As a child she learned that her security rested on 'repression' of all feelings. Her acceptability then depended on her being 'emotionless'. But feelings arise spontaneously and at thirty years of age she now had a huge flood of repressed feelings within her, needing to be seen and responded to, but which sub-consciously were seen as life-threatening. It was not 'flooding the house' that accounted for her compulsive behaviour but 'the flood of emotions' within her. As she gradually learned to express the different feelings, the obsessive-compulsive behaviours began to extinguish.

The tormented life of persons with obsessive-compulsive problems is illustrated in the following poem:-

COMPULSIONS

Checking, checking, checking,
twisting, twisting, twisting,
tight, tight, tight,
faster, faster, faster,
ah! all is right
no, no, check again
just one more run,
back, back, back,

lights, doors, taps,
switches, windows, gas.
Sleep, sleep, sleep,
ease, ease, ease,
no don't doze,
rise up once more,
no flood, no waste,
no light, no fire,
no flow,
no row,
no openness,
emotionless,
or world will cease.

Washing, washing, washing,
scrubbing, scrubbing, scrubbing,
five times,
how many times
no start again
one, two, three,
four, five, see
criss cross,
up and down
step missed
start again
skin raw raw
bleeding, bleeding, bleeding,
no matter
do over and over.

Rubbing, rubbing, rubbing,
safe, safe, safe,
clean, clean, clean,
who sat there
did he touch there
did I touch here
wash, wash, wash,

scrub, scrub, scrub,
rash, rash, rash,
dirt, dirt, dirt,
unclean, unclean, unclean,
worthless, worthless, worthless,
never ending search,
spotless, spotless, spotless,
hateful, hateful, hateful
impure, impure, impure
who could ever love me?

You can see now that the second requirement for giving and receiving staff support is complex and that most of us have difficulties in the expression of both welfare and emergency feelings. Nonetheless, the way forward is the awareness that all feelings are positive and that owning, valuing, respecting and constructively expressing feelings will led to a resolution of personal and interpersonal issues.

C. Dependency Versus Independence

There is a notion about that never asking for help means being independent and that to do the contrary means being dependent. Is this true? Hardly, as many of your needs are met in relationships - such as the need for affection, support, knowledge, expertise, advice, warmth, friendship, companionship, sexual gratification and it is then a matter of survival and personal development for you to express these needs. When you do not ask for support or help then surely this is an act of neglect of self . Ask yourself what is it that blocks you from making a request: Is it fear of rejection, of being judged, criticised or disapproved of? If it is then your reticence is an act of dependency and not at all one of independence. Independence means making the request for support or whatever you want and being independent of the response of the receiver. For example if you make a request of someone but expect him to say 'yes' and react negatively when he says 'no' then you are being dependent on him; expecting him to take responsibility for you. Remember a request is not a command. When you are independent you want the other person to be free to respond to your request and you value his 'no' in the same way as you would value his 'yes' response. Independence is then being able to seek and receive help and support but allowing the other person freedom of response. Dependency, on the other hand means either not expressing the need for help or support or asking in a commanding rather than requesting manner. It is interesting that when you ask people how they feel when somebody asks for help, the usual response is "I feel pleased and affirmed to be asked". But when you reverse the question - "Do you go to others for help?" - the usual response is 'no' because the expectation of how others will receive the request does not mirror people's own experience of being pleased when someone approaches them.

In all relationships it is important that we go to each other for care, affirmation, advice and support.

It is even more important within the context of a stressful occupation that mutual support and help becomes an everyday experience. Within any staff group there are huge resources of help, creativity, wisdom, support and affirmation available; the sad thing is that such resources often lie untapped.

4. STAFF MORALE

The bedrock of the creation of a supportive staff environment is staff morale. Staff morale is the lifeblood of any staff group. Its promotion is the responsibility of all members of staff but it is particularly important that principals and vice-principals be active in its development; without their visible encouragement and participation it is unlikely to develop.

There are five main requirements for the creation of positive staff morale:

A. High level of interaction among staff

B. Decisions are made by the group

C. Leaders are available and approachable

D. Leaders affirm staff and staff affirm each other

E. Staff affirm leaders

A. Levels of Staff Interaction among Staff

The first requirement indicates that the more interaction that occurs between staff the better the morale. Some staffs have a situation where members pass each other like ships in the night, never interacting. The more varied the interactions the better: social, problem-solving, support, affirmation, planning, care, creative, sport. It is important that the principal notices the teacher(s) who absents himself or herself from such interactions. Generally, such withdrawal is indicative of vulnerability and feelings of threat and a discreet, caring, concerned approach to this teacher is needed. Equally, the teacher who over dominates staff-interactions needs to be delicately approached. Both of these teachers can unwittingly make the development of good staff morale difficult. Both need help and understanding.

B. Decision-Making

The second requirement centres on decision-making. I once mentioned to a group of over 500 primary school teachers that one of my experiences in going around to many school staffs was that some principals hid themselves away in their offices and classrooms and only emerged to give instructions and commands and that staff meetings were a rare phenomenon. There was a loud cheer from the audience which suggested that my observation was not unfounded. It is also the experience of some staffs that when staff meetings are convened, decisions have already been made by the principal before (s)he comes to the meeting and that they are not included in the decision making. This is an unwise practice as decisions which have not evolved from consultation with staff are likely to receive poor cooperation and can sometimes be sabotaged, and rightly so! Decisions, which are not inclusive of staff, are abusive and non-respecting of the staff's right to be participants in the decision making process. Decisions which arise from joint-decision making are far more likely to be acted upon as staff members feel they are part of that decision and feel affirmed and respected by the consultation process. Regular, well-organised, goal-directed staff meetings are a must for the creation of good morale. Meetings for the sake of meetings only create frustration and annoyance and weaken morale.

C. Leader Availability

Effective leadership is an essential aspect of an effective school and will be dealt with in more detail in the chapter on the school. It has relevance here in that availability and approachability of the principal and vice-principal are important factors in the creation of positive staff morale. Many principals complain that one of their major tasks is dealing with a demoralised teaching staff who have lost motivation, initiative and who are no longer challenged within their profession. Not an easy task! It is important that principals give very clear non-verbal and verbal messages of availability. Apart from crisis situations it is good to specify times that are most convenient. Even more important is communicating approachability. Non-verbal language speaks volumes on this issue: lack of eye contact, talking 'on the run', speeded conversations, clock-watching, irritablity, severe facial expressions, restlessness - all send messages of unapproachability. Further indicators of unapproachability include not listening, not showing interest in colleagues' personal lives, not exhibiting concern either during staff members' personal or professional crises, not delegating, not seeking their opinions, not seeking help for self, blaming, criticising, not relating on first name terms. Approachability is conveyed through good eye-contact, listening, concern, sensitivity to the stresses and strains teachers may be experiencing, personal time with each member of staff, requesting support and help, admitting one's own vulnerabilities and active response to teachers' requests for help and support.

D. Affirmation of Staff

The fourth requirement is connected with the issue of affirmation. Because few of us have reached the peaks of high self-esteem, affirmation from colleagues and leaders aids the growth of self-esteem. Even when you have high self-esteem, affirmation is a bonus to be enjoyed. Most of us still have needs for recognition and approval. The difficulty arises if the needs are dependency needs when criticism or the absence of affirmation then become severe blows to self-esteem, and, in turn, badly affect staff morale. Recognition, respect, valuing, affirming, encouragement, praise are not regular features of staff/staff or leader/staff interactions. What is more common is criticism, avoidance, silence, negative gossip and 'put-down' messages. All of the latter damage self-esteem and staff morale. It is the responsibility of all members of staff and, again, especially leaders, to develop the art of affirmation. Giving affirmation is a subtle, delicate issue but when done well has many rewarding consequences.
Guidelines for giving affirmations are as follows:

Giving Affirmations

● *Only ever give honest and genuine affirmations.*
If you are not genuine and sincere about a positive affirmation and you do not really feel that the person deserves it, your non-verbal language will give you away and your affirmation will be rejected as insincere.

● *Give an affirmation without expectation of a receptive response.*
Generally it is true to say that when a person reacts defensively to a positive affirmation it means that the person needs more affirmations. Do not give up - remember that affirmation is an expression of something you feel and perceive and must not be given to gain

a particular response. In the end the other person will see your genuineness and be affirmed by it.

●*The best affirmation is undivided attention to the other person.*
Avoid effusive compliments (they are rarely genuine). A look, a nod, a smile may be sufficient to affirm a colleague. Always be sure full attention is given.

● *Be sure the affirmation is unconditional and has no ulterior motive.*
Do not give an affirmation to get something back (like an affirmation in return, praise or a favour) - that is manipulation and not affirmation.

●*Give affirmations frequently to create a mutual cycle of affirming between members of a staff.*

●*Do not employ cliches, jargon and popular superlatives ('Great!', 'Super!', 'Terrific!', 'A1!'); be yourself and be genuine.*

● *Spontaneous unconditional affirmations are the most powerful.*

● *Focus your affirmations on an area that is important to your colleague.*
Look for signs from the person of what is important to them. Possible considerations are dress, work, verbal language, body language, origin, social, cultural and educational background, knowledge of a specific topic, interests, hobbies, social behaviour and also what you hear from the students, colleagues, friends and partner of the person to whom you want to give affirmations.

E. Constructive Feedback on Differences

Feedback on differences between you and a colleague is easier to give and more likely to be received within a context of regular mutual affirmation.

Giving positive affirmations generally comes more easily to people than communicating on differences, on unmet needs and on emergency feelings such as anger or resentment. There are some guidelines which may help when you need to give such feedback:

● *Rarely to a person with low self-esteem*
An affirming relationship with this person would need to be established before (s)he would be in a position not to perceive such feedback as threatening to self-esteem but to see it as purely an expression of something going on for the person giving the feedback.

● *Never in the presence of others*
This is a wise stipulation whether one is giving feedback or expressing reservations or asserting that a particular behaviour on the other person's part (principal, colleague, student) is not acceptable to you. It is best to do so privately and discreetly and always within the context of a valuing, respecting regard for the other person.

● *Given as soon as possible*
Delayed feedback on, for example, dissatisfaction or misgivings only leads to a build-up of tension within you and can later on often lead to an out-of-proportion expression of the issue that was bothering you. Nevertheless, as indicated, timing and place of feedback are all important and these issues must be taken into consideration. The rule of thumb is to bring up your 'emergency' issue as soon as possible but in a place and at a time when it is least likely to create conflict between you and the other person.

● *Clear and specific in your communication of your conflict*
Many people tend to be general in their expression of unmet needs and dissatisfactions. For example, for a teacher to say to a principal, "I get no back-up or support in this school" is too general. What precisely is your need? Is it "I need help and support to deal with student A from you as principal and from the other teachers who have this student in their classes". The latter is much more specific and further questioning will clarify what exactly is the nature of the

conflict the teacher has with the particular student and what remedial actions are needed - on the part of the teacher himself or herself, on the part of the principal and the other teachers and on the part of the student. It may well be that parents may need to be involved as back-up reinforcers of school policy.

● *Outline the consequence of the problematic behaviour*
In the last example above, the consequences of student A's problematic behaviours in the classroom may be that the teacher spends half of the class time trying to control the student and that the rest of the class is losing out on valuable learning time. Other consequences may be that the teacher is stressed, losing motivation and self-esteem and is undermined and that negative attitudes to students and teaching are developing. It is a worrying issue that many teachers are accepting that the rise in problems in the classroom are going to continue to escalate to proportions similar to some schools in America where the corridors are patrolled by policemen. I believe that that evolution is not inevitable. Quite the contrary; the problems manifesting themselves within our educational system are revelations about the unmet needs of people within the systems - of the teachers, of the students coming from different educational, social, emotional and cultural backgrounds, of the principals and vice-principals, of the different Church bodies and Boards of Management bodies. The problems are also a revelation about the unmet needs of people who are outside the system but who are, nonetheless, deeply affected by the educational system - people such as parents, employers, politicians, psychologists, social workers, medical personnel, community associations and trade unions. The problems are not only a revelation about unmet needs but present an opportunity and a challenge to creatively respond at the educational, psychological, social, and political levels to these manifestations. It is important that these problems, which are signals of unmet educational, psychological and social needs, are not flown in vain. It is not the brief of this book to answer these issues but much of what is said about more positive approaches to teaching does embrace a radical view of education and one that I believe would need to be included in the response to the multiple

problems within our educational system today.

● *Stick to the issue on hand*
Bringing into the discussion issues from the past escalates conflict. "Going into the museum and pulling out all the old skeletons of the past" which are not relevant to the issue in hand will only cloud the issue and, generally, cause more hurt, anger and confusion. Do not allow the other person or do not allow yourself to drift from the present-moment issue that you are concerned to talk out openly and to reach some resolution. There is a technique which is called the 'broken-record' which simply means repeating as often as is needed your feelings and unmet need on a particular issue. Taking up a previous example on not being consulted - "John, when decisions are made on issues relating to my work and I haven't been consulted, I feel angry and I am asking that in future that I be consulted on such matters" - if John replies "I'm very busy, you know, lots of things on my mind", the appropriate response is "I understand you're busy but when decisions are made.....". This process is repeated until you feel heard and a reasonable resolution has been reached.

● *Keep behaviour and person separate*
Do not confuse the behaviour which is a source of conflict for you with the person who is engaging in the behaviour. "Play the ball and not the behaviour". As indicated, what we typically do is label a person so that the person feels put down, judged and criticised. An insensitive remark becomes "you're so insensitive" or a child not making a responsible effort becomes "you're lazy" or a principal who does not listen to a staff member's needs becomes 'he is impossible to talk to". Labelling creates defensiveness and undermines the self-esteem of the receiver of your message. State specifically the 'bit' of behaviour that is causing difficulty for you and show how it blocks a particular need of yours.

● *Only use first-hand information*

● *Agree how to avoid repetitions*

● *'When it's over - never bring it up again'*

F. Affirmation of Leaders

The guidelines outlined above regarding affirmations and bringing up 'difficult' issues apply to the relationship between staff and principals and vice-principals. Who affirms the leaders is an important issue! Very often staff are aware of their own needs for recognition and approval but forget that leaders have similar needs. Again, a cycle of staff/leader affirmation is likely to be reciprocated by leader/staff recognition and approval.

5. PROBLEM-SOLVING

Within any social system problems arise. When such problems are not resolved the system is said to be dysfunctional, whereas when problems are responded to as challenges to improve relationships and resources within the troubled system, and are resolved, the system is said to be functional. What is interesting is that healthy systems (eg. family, classroom, school, staff, community associations) appear to go through a process of problem-solving involving, without realisation, a step-by-step approach, whereas dysfunctional systems may not even get to the first step of problem-solving which is identification of the problem. There are different problem-solving methods. The method suggested below is a seven step method.

a. Identification of the Problem

It is useful to catalogue problems into **instrumental** and **affective**. **Instrumental** problems are connected with resources and responsibilities. Typical instrumental problems within many schools are overcrowded classrooms, lack of secretarial assistance, lack of teaching tools, curriculum issues, problems in assignment of classes. **Affective** problems embrace personal and interpersonal emotional and behavioural problems. Examples of the latter include a principal who is over-dominating or controlling or passive and non-assertive; teachers having classroom management problems; a teacher with a personal problem of anxiety, depression, dependency on alcohol; high absenteeism of a teacher or pupil; student who is shy and withdrawn; student who is aggressive and non-cooperative within the classrooms.

An important element of this first step in problem-solving is "who" identifies the problem. Sometimes, if it is a student who identifies the problem, (s)he may not be taken seriously and the teacher's judgement is often given more credence. If it is a parent who identifies the problem - for example, a teacher who is critical and aggressive within a classroom - then what frequently happens is that teachers become defensive and do not respond positively to the identified problem. If it is another teacher who identifies the problematic behaviour of a colleague, often that teacher may not pursue the issue or may report the matter to the principal, who may, in turn, drop the matter. What a pity! Everybody now loses out - the school, the teacher who is not coping, the teacher who identified the problem, the students and the principal who is not exercising his or her leadership role.

Instrumental problems tend to be far more frequently identified within school and classroom systems. Affective issues tend to be much more threatening to an individual's self-esteem and, consequently, tend to be denied, suppressed or projected onto others. Sometimes the high emotional responses shown to instrumental issues, for example, assignment of classes and hours, mask deeper affective problems within staff such as rivalry, resentment of nepotism, threat of failure, anger at not being consulted.

The important factor to be alert to when a problem is identified, whether affective or instrumental, is the emotional 'loading' that surrounds the problem; primarily identifiable in the non-verbal behaviours of the people concerned. Examples of these non-verbal signs are facial expression, tone of voice, loudness of voice, nervous mannerisms, lack of eye contact, and body posture. Try to get to the feelings behind people's responses as this reveals the seriousness of the issue for them.

b. Communication of the Problem

It is quite amazing what can happen at this stage of problem-solving. Very often nothing happens. The person who has identified the problem says nothing to anybody. Many students never reveal to the principal or other teachers or to their parents victimisation by a particular teacher or group of peers. Similarly, there are teachers who are aware that a colleague is having serious difficulties within the classroom or is very fearful of a principal but do nothing about it. Typical outcomes that develop following problem identification are gossip or complaining, or resignation that nothing can be done, or blaming - none of which is constructive. It is important when a problem is identified that it is communicated to a source who can either advise what can be done or respond directly to the problem issues. Remember everybody benefits when a problem is positively responded to and the problem is not an indictment of another person but an opportunity for growth within a system.

c. Brainstorming Solutions to the Problem

This is the most creative and dynamic step in the problem-solving process. It is where everybody concerned with the problem looks for solutions; the idea being to suggest any notion that comes into your head that might resolve the problem. It is important that all the individuals whom the problem affects be involved. Unfortunately, in many schools students are often not included in this process even though its outcome may directly affect them. A teacher having problems of management within a particular classroom would be wise to include all the members of that class in the brainstorming session. Sometimes parents may need to be invited in to give their suggestions for change.

An essential aspect of brainstorming is that there must be no judging or criticism of proferred solutions no matter how off the wall you may feel they are. Any judgement during brainstorming will quickly dry up creativity as people are not willing to risk the humiliation of being ridiculed. It is easy to see how a verbal judgement such as "That's a load of rubbish" will sabotage brain-storming but much more subtle non-verbal messages like sighing or 'tch tching' or a smile at another across the room, or the raising of eyebrows can be equally devastating.

All solutions must be written down and efforts continually affirmed.

d. Selection of an Option

This can be the most difficult step as differences between problem-solvers are much more likely to appear at this point. It is always difficult to choose a solution that will suit everybody. Because of the latter very often a stalemate can come about. Consideration of two issues will make it less likely for entrenched positions to develop: one is the instrumental factor of what has to be done, and second is the affective or relationship factor which has to do with who will benefit from a commitment to a proposed solution. If one only considers the 'what', people can be resistant to taking on more responsibilities but when relationships are also considered people tend to be more amenable to adopting a solution that will be of considerable help to a colleague or a student or a principal. For example, I may not be having any difficulty with classroom management and I am not enamoured with a proposed alternative management system which is going to make some demands on me. At an instrumental level the proposed option does not appeal but when I consider that it may greatly help a troubled colleague and students who may be exploiting a teacher's vulnerabilities, I am much more likely to commit myself to the solution. If I do not I seriously need to ask myself "What is blocking me from helping a colleague or student who is in obvious distress?".

e. Action

This is the most important step as all the words in the world do not change situations but actions can and do. Sometimes, in spite of going through all the previous steps, nothing happens or only half-hearted efforts are made or commendable efforts are made but peter out after a short time. An insurance against the latter outcome is an **accountability system**. Accountability is not a policing system but a method of ensuring the continuance of action through feedback, encouragement and support. The idea is that responsibilities are divided out between the members of a problem-solving group and either individuals or groups of individuals meet at set times and places to report to each other on progress and on any difficulties that may have arisen. For example, if four groups are formed then A reports to B, B to C, C to A, D to B. This accountability system must be well organised and executed.

f. Monitor Progress of Action

Is the execution of the option chosen having any effect? Let us assume that participants are truly trying but only a little change is occurring. It may well be that more or different action is needed so that a return to step D. is needed for the selection of yet another option. If, on implementation of this added option, nothing much changes, then the wrong problem or only a surface problem which was masking a deeper issue, may have been identified. A return to step A. will be required in order to identify the real problem. As already pointed out, very often instrumental issues mask deeper affective issues. An example of this has happened in schools which are an amalgamation of two or three schools in a local area, where conflict on instrumental issues, on deeper investigation, reveals hidden fears of one group not feeling valued by the other staff members of what was the more desirable school in the local area. Similar affective difficulties may arise when an all male school staff joins an all female school staff. Other affective issues are that teachers of the so-called 'less important' subjects (like religion, domestic science, civics) often feel less recognised and valued in the school system. Indeed, subjects like religion and civics have become the hardest to teach because they are not examination courses and motivation to listen and learn is not high among students. I know of many religion and civics teachers who have management problems in classrooms. Also, Irish has become a difficult subject to teach because of poor motivation and its relevance not being appreciated. All these difficulties need to be recognised within a school system and corrective actions taken with the support of all staff.

g. Evaluation of Problem-Solving Strategy

The main purpose of this step is to bring the lessons of the present problem-solving experience into future resolutions of other issues which will inevitably arise. It is not the case that problems will ever be totally resolved within educational systems. New problems will arise in response to changing economic, social, moral, religious, political and psychological circumstances within the wider society. These problems are challenges to the educational system to respond to different needs that have emerged in the population of students, teachers, managers, parents and employers who either directly or indirectly use the systems.

Previous experience of conflict-resolution aids future resolution of difficulties when the insights and effective strategies gained are brought to bear on the new problem/challenge. Beware though of assuming that what worked before will work again.

6. RESPONDING TO RIGIDITY

A difficult aspect of the development of healthy staff relationships is coping with a principal or colleague who is inflexible and rigid in his or her behaviour. People with such problematic behaviour live their lives according to numerous laws of 'shoulds', 'should not's', 'have to's', 'musts' and 'ought to's'. It was one of the very few times that Christ got angry in the Gospels when he said to the Pharisees "You make it as if man is made for the law but man is greater than the law and the law is there for man to use wisely and compassionately". At another time, Christ said "All laws are put aside; all man needs to do is love God with all his heart and love his neighbour as himself". The latter, the love of self, was the best kept secret in the Catholic Church. How wise of Christ to see that when man truly values himself, others and his universe, there is no need for laws. The problem in many countries, and many social systems (family, school, classroom, partnership, business organisations) is that people do not respect and value each other. When that is the case laws, rules and regulations evolve as protectors against neglect, abuse, exploitation and rejection.

To be able to cope and respond effectively to the person exhibiting a rigid approach to issues demands an indepth understanding of the nature and function of rigidity. A case study will help to clarify this issue. This was a young Science teacher, in his late twenties, who was referred to me with high blood pressure and stomach ulcers - serious signs of stress. The nature of his rigidity was that he had to be the 'perfect' teacher. He spent hours preparing classes because he had to know everything and to be able to answer any questions from students in the classroom. He spent the entire school day writing work for the students on the blackboard - leaving no room for mistakes or control difficulties in the classroom! Any extra curricular activities that needed to be done in the school he would volunteer to do and he would do them perfectly. Quite innocently be boasted to me that since he had taken over the Vincent de Paul Fund in the school he had collected more money than anyone before. You might say what a prize this man was for the school. However, the effects on him were life-threatening and, no doubt, he was projecting his own irrational standards onto students, thereby putting them under pressure. Before he went to school each morning, he used literally get sick with the dread and worry about the day: "Will I manage; will I remember everything I've prepared; will I be able to control the class; will I be approved by colleagues and principal?" These high anxieties pushed his blood pressure up and 'knotted' his stomach. Of course, he let nobody see these vulnerabilities. Though sick he would never be absent. In all his eight years of teaching he had never missed a day.

Now all human behaviour has a function but what possibly could be the purpose of such rigidity and inflexibility? The answer is **protection.** His rigidity is a protection against multiple fears of failure, criticism, rejection. How clever to develop rigid attitudes of perfectionism as 'If I'm perfect in all that I do, how can I then experience failure, criticism or rejection?". Indeed, how could you, except that it is impossible to be perfect in behaviour at all times and hence the anxiety that his defense behaviours might not be strong enough. Nonetheless, the strategy works most of the time. But why is this young man, very intellectually able, living life in constant fear and rigidity? Fears arise from dependency. Clearly he is very dependent on approval and acceptance from others and on success. But take it a step deeper, why is he so dependent? The answer to this is that he has little regard for himself, deeply doubts his capabilities - in short, he has low self-esteem. And one more step, whence the low self-esteem? Low self-esteem, as you have seen, comes from unresolved conflicts in childhood. No matter how well he did as a child, whether it was academically, athletically or otherwise, the response from both his parents was "Well, you could have done better".

The clear message he got in these early years of his life is "You are never good enough". What a sad legacy to give a child! He now develops no inner conviction of his own worthiness, remains dependent and fearful of other people's judgements (parents and others). Now we see the wisdom of the rigid attitudes; it is as if he is saying to his parents: "If I'm perfect will you now love and approve of me?". **Rigid behaviours are always protectors - weapons against hurt and rejection.** To try and take away a person's rigidity without understanding its purpose will always fail. People who are rigid in attitudes and behaviour become even more so when confronted, the reason being that they are afraid of losing the weapon that protects them. The problem is that the weapon puts psychological and physical health at risk.

In order to know how best to respond to a person who is behaviourly rigid and inflexible, it is useful to illustrate the above process of the development of rigid attitudes and behaviours.

It can be seen from the outline below that rigidity masks emotional problems and the focus of response to the person displaying rigid cognitive and behavioural patterns with consequent physical complaints, must be at the emotional levels. To move in at the cognitive or behavioural levels would mean risking losing contact with the person as these levels are protectors of low self-esteem and will only weaken when self-esteem elevates. When self-

EMOTIONAL	Unresolved Childhood Conflicts (Conditionality or total neglect)
	↕
EMOTIONAL	Low Self-Esteem (I am not good enough for my parents/others)
	↕
EMOTIONAL	Dependency (I need to be valued and approved by parents/others)
	↕
EMOTIONAL	Fears of Rejection, Disapproval, Criticism, Failure.
	↕
COGNITIVE	Rigid Attitudes (People should accept me, I should be perfect in what I do, I shouldn't fail ......)
	↕
BEHAVIOURAL	Rigid Behaviours (Over-working, imbalanced lifestyle, not listening to feedback, authoritarianism, passive-manipulation....)
	↕
PHYSICAL	Psychosomatic Complaints (Heart disease, blood pressure, stomach problems, headaches..............)

esteem rises, dependency and fears reduce and the need for protectors in the form of rigidities disappears. The staff member or student who is regarded as 'rigid' and 'impossible' needs attending to self-esteem through affirmation, affection, encouragement, support and, most of all, belief in their worthiness in terms of their lovability and capability. To put it in short terms the person needs to be unconditionally valued.

Any system wherein a person or different groups of people do not value each other gives rise to rigid 'protective' patterns of behaviours.

It is encumbent on all members of such a system to create a social and emotional environment wherein members will not have to protect themselves from disrespect, hurt and rejection but feel safe and secure in the evident value that each member shows to the other.

7. KEY ISSUES

a. Staff relationships are a major source of stress within the school system.

b. It is of significance to all members of staff when a colleague has a self-esteem problem.

c. Defensive, unsupportive patterns of communication are the most common forms of relating in staffrooms.

d. Communication is primarily about revealing and getting one's needs met. Many needs are not met because of dysfunctional communication.

e. Vulnerability and weaknesses are **strengths.**

f. There are **Welfare** feelings and **Emergency** feelings and both are positive.

g. Never asking for help is an act of dependency .

h. Staff-morale is the life-blood of a school's staff group.

i. Problem-solving approaches are an inherent part of effective social systems.

j. Rigidity is a symptom of emotional insecurity.

8. KEY TASKS

a.   Development of open/relating patterns of communication which are:-
- Non-judgemental
- Permissive
- Spontaneous
- Empathic
- Egalitarian
- Provisional

creates a supportive and positive school environment wherein teachers can feel safe in voicing and getting help and support for their difficulties.

b.   Send an "I" message that is direct and clear when expressing any need.

c.   Seeking and receiving help and support need to be part of the daily working routine.

d.   Express all feelings in full openness.

e.   Be independent by seeking help and support when you need it and allow the receiver freedom to say "yes" or "no".

f.   Create positive staff morale through:
- A high level of staff interaction
- Group decision-making
- Leader availability and approachability
- Leader and staff affirmation of staff
- Staff affirmation of leaders
- Constructive communication of differences, unmet needs and emergency feelings.

g.   Development of an effective problem-solving approach to conflict issues.

Main steps are :

- Identification of problem
- Communication of problem to knowledgeable source
- Brainstorming solutions
- Selection of options
- Action
- Monitor
- Evaluation

Remember that many conflicts on instrumental issues mask deeper affective conflicts.

h.   The staff member or student who displays rigidity needs affirmation, affection, recognition, support, encouragement and belief in their worthiness.

CHAPTER FOUR

The Student

1. MALADAPTIVE BEHAVIOUR IS ALWAYS RIGHT

2. SIGNS OF STUDENTS' EMOTIONAL CONFLICTS

3. TEACHER/STUDENT RELATIONSHIPS

      a. Absence of Relationship
      b. Relationship Devoid of Feelings
      c. Narcissistic Relationship
      d. Over-involved Relationship
      e. Symbiotic Relationship
      f. Empathic Relationship

4. STUDENT SELF-ESTEEM IN THE CLASSROOM

      A. Identifying Students with Low
         Self-Esteem
      B. Self-Esteem and Learning
      C. Increasing Self-Esteem in the Classroom

5. KEY ISSUES

6. KEY TASKS

1. MALADAPTIVE BEHAVIOUR IS ALWAYS RIGHT

Students presenting with behavioural difficulties within the class-room and school corridors have become a major source of stress in teaching. In most cases an authoritarian response to these students no longer works and neither is it desirable. Authoritarianism dehumanises and blocks the mature development of children. Many schools and individual teachers have not discovered constructive approaches to disruptive behaviours within classrooms. A full understanding of the nature of pupils' maladaptive behaviours can lead to the development of appropriate responses to them.

The first insight that is needed is that **students' maladaptive behaviour is always right**. Sounds like a paradox, does it not? How could behaviour like fidgetting, inattentiveness, aggressive outbursts, insolence, refusals to do work, temper tantrums and so on be right? The issue is that these behaviours are **symptoms or signs of underlying conflicts within the child**. They are not the problem but revelations or manifestations of it. Unfortunately, because these behavioural manifestations disrupt your teaching they become problems to you and indeed to other students. The reaction is to punish them. However, in spite of the punishments, the behaviours will tend to persist, because you have not identified the core of the problem and your punishing response will only aggravate that unidentified problem. Let us take some examples. I remember being invited into a primary school in England to deal with a child who was causing serious behavioural difficulties within the classroom. I got to the school before classes started and the child was pointed out to me by his class teacher as he filed past us into the classroom. He was displaying no maladaptive behaviours at that moment. I noticed that this seven year old child was quite small and thin for his age, somewhat pale and emaciated, clothing dishevelled and as he passed me by there was a strong smell of urine from the child. I had agreed with the principal and class teacher that I would sit at the back of the class and observe this child. Once children get into classroom they tend to forget about the existence of an observer. The child, let us call him Mark, went to his desk, took his books out of his bag and put them into his desk. When the class was requested to take out a particular book he duly complied. For about fifteen minutes the child cooperated with the teaching demands but then, very audibly, began to make noises with the flap of his desk. Immediately the teacher came down to him and said "stop that noise Mark". A few minutes later when her attention was off him he pulled at the student in front of him. Once again the teacher came down to him and corrected him. This cycle of maladaptive behaviours and teacher's correction of them continued for the rest of the class up to the eleven o'clock break. The teacher spent much of her class time correcting Mark's disruptive behaviour. However, her ridiculing and scolding were having little or no impact.

Surely you will say that the teacher had to do what she was doing? My point is that no understanding of the child's maladaptive behaviour is present in her response to its appearance. I had already guessed what was the deeper issue. I enquired from the principal and class teacher about the home circumstances of the child. It transpired he was from a broken home. Father had left three years before and had maintained no contact with the family. Mother was under considerable stress, working in a factory, and very impatient and irritable with her son. She was gone to work before be left for school and the child was not being fed in the mornings; neither was he being washed. I also discovered he was a bed-wetter. After school the child often had to sit outside his home for a number of hours before his mother came home. I explained to the class teacher and principal that the child's maladaptive behaviours were a sign of an underlying conflict of not feeling wanted and that he had a massive unmet need to be seen and loved. I also pointed out that unless these underlying needs were met in the classroom it was unlikely that progress would be made in reducing his disruptive behaviours. I further illustrated that the disruptive behaviours were gaining him some attention but that when he engaged in responsible behaviours no response was given. I suggested that the major response that the child needed was for his class teacher to develop an affirming, valuing and close relationship with him. Such a relationship would meet his unmet needs and reduce this child's conflict of not feeling wanted. I also stressed that when the child engaged in responsible behaviours that these should get immediate reinforcing responses from the teacher. Such a strategy would lead to an increase in responsible actions and a corresponding decrease in the disruptive ones. I also advised that the disruptive actions should be ignored as much as possible and when this was not possible, should be corrected in a firm but positive manner. The class teacher quickly saw how she had been unwittingly increasing the child's maladaptive behaviours and she also saw the wisdom of attending to the child's responsible behaviours. She adopted this policy and there was a considerable improvement in the child's behaviour within the classroom. The teacher resisted the notion of the need for a close relationship with the child. Her response to this request was "I treat all the children in the classroom in the same way". I said that would be fine if all the children were the same but the fact is that this child does need help because of his unfortunate circumstances. She confessed she could not warm to the child. I also arranged help for the mother and, with her agreement, had the child washed and fed when he came to school. The principal agreed to give more attention to the child. It was interesting that the following September, the child entered a new class to a teacher who established a very warm affirming relationship with him. He manifested no difficulties during his year with her.

To say that maladaptive behaviours are 'right' is correct because they manifest the inner conflicts of children. Nevertheless, the same behaviours are also 'unacceptable' because they disrupt classes and schools and also because they are not desirable or adaptive ways to getting needs met. However, it is important to realise that the child **is not deliberately** engaging in these behaviours but knows of no other way to get his or her needs met. More than likely adaptive ways did not work in the home for the child and, in desperation, the maladaptive ways developed as a last resort. More importantly, the maladaptive behaviours are signs and these must not be shown in vain by the child. What is also important is that the underlying issue is different for each child so that there is no general way of responding to an individual child's conflict. What I have learned in helping children, adolescents and adults over the years is that each person who comes to me for help needs a different therapy.

A relevant question is why do we refer to children's disruptive behaviours as maladaptive? Take a child who is very clinging so that he goes around pulling on his mother's skirt all day. In what way is the behaviour maladaptive? It is maladaptive because it never resolves the child's underlying conflict and, indeed, often exacerbates it. When a child constantly clings, very often the parent will get irritated and push the child away with a scolding remark "stop pulling out of me". Such a response plunges the child back into his frightening conviction that he is not loved and so the conflict increases and perpetuates. Similarly, children or adolescents who steal are very often manifesting hurt and anger because many of their rights to be loved, cared for, nurtured, protected, given freedom and challenged, were stolen from them by parents who either badly neglected or over controlled and dominated them. Unfortunately, the stealing results in further condemnation by parents and so the hidden conflict remains.

The understanding of students' maladaptive behaviours can be illustrated as follows:

Maladaptive Behaviours   *LEVEL 1*
↕
Signs   *LEVEL 2*
↕
Unique Underlying Conflicts   *LEVEL 3*
↕
Demanding Unique Responses from Parents/Teachers/ Significant Others.

The responses of parents, teachers and other significant adults to the child's conflicts must occur at all levels; focusing on level 1 without identifying or responding to level 3 is unlikely to be successful. The rest of this chapter suggests ways of responding at level 3; the next chapter concentrates on level 1.

2. SIGNS OF STUDENTS' EMOTIONAL CONFLICTS

It is not difficult for teachers to identify the at risk child. There are multiple manifestations of the unmet needs of children. When such behavioural manifestations are regularly shown then appropriate and constructive responses are needed in the classroom and school with back-up from the family system. Typical signs of child or adolescent distress within classroom or school settings are outlined below. A student who is regularly showing two or more of these behaviours is manifesting clear signs of emotional conflict.

Signs of Emotional Conflict

When you read through the list below you will notice that the signs of emotional conflict among children have been categorised under three main headings: physical, under-control, and over-control signs. The physical signs are common to those students who manifest problematic responses under either of the other two categories. Signs of under-control are those behaviours that can be very troublesome to others but are, nonetheless, clear signs of emotional disturbance. The student acts out of his or her inner conflicts in a sub-conscious attempt to get his or her needs met. Typical under-control behaviours are aggressiveness, insolence, bullying and hyperactivity. Psychologically these behaviours are saying something 'right' about the student but socially the behaviours can make it very difficult to teach a class or manage a school. Because these under-control behaviours are socially unacceptable then some action is needed to either reduce or extinguish their occurence (see next chapter). However, the latter must only be done in the context of an attempt to discover the psychological 'rightness' of these upsetting manifestations. It is interesting and also understandable that children who exhibit under-control behaviours are those with the highest referrals to principals, school counsellors and back-up psychological and social services. It is also of note that boys compared to girls are more likely to manifest their inner conflicts via under-control behaviours.

More girls than boys engage in over-control behaviours but many boys do so also - again in a sub-conscious effort to have their emotional problems seen. Over-control problem behaviours, such as shyness, over-diligence, perfectionism do not in any serious way upset social systems such as the classroom or school. The quiet, withdrawn child does not interfere with classroom work and very often such a child is not seen as problematic and does not get the help that (s)he needs. Unfortunately, these children are often more at risk than their peers who 'act out' their problems. It is as if those who shout the loudest are the ones more likely to be heard. It is important therefore that teachers be vigilant for the over-control signs of emotional conflict. The signs of under-control do not need such vigilance as they will very strongly wake you up to the presence of students who have unmet emotional needs. The hope is that both sets of children will have their needs detected and appropriately responded to and that more adaptive ways of getting their needs met will be taught to them. There is no doubt that teachers are becoming more aware of and more concerned about the emotional and social welfare of their students and want to learn how to create a healthy emotional climate within the classroom and school.

A. Physical Signs

Nail-biting, facial grimacing, restlessness, stammering, sudden blushing or paling, frequent twitching of muscles, poor physical co-ordination, bed-wetting, soiling, frequent complaints of head-aches, stomach aches or other pains, obesity, loss of weight, poor appetite, jumping at sudden noises, loss of energy, affectations or posturings.

B. Signs of Under-Control
● **Personal Signs: Student**
Behaviour too young for age, hyperactivity, irresponsible behaviour, impulsiveness, little academic effort, mischieviousness, inability to work alone, over excitable, uncontrolled laughing or giggling, high distractability, extravagant emotional expression, frequent nightmares, marked pressure of ideas that crowd forward so

fast that one sentence is left unfinished as another is begun, destructiveness of school property, defacing of books, abusive or obscene language, writing obscenities on walls, frequent minor delinquencies - lying, cheating, thieving, hatred of school work, does not learn from experience, highly favours out-of-class activities, blaming of others for mistakes and failures, highly critical of others, show-off, truanting from school.

● **Interpersonal Signs: Teacher**
Frequent requests for help, attention-seeking, crushes on teachers, effort to curry favour with teacher, staying persistently after class to talk with teacher, frequently disruptive in class, many requests for special attentions and favours, irrelevant answers to questions, acting tough in class, exaggerated courtesy, constant bragging, inability to take criticism, frequent justification of self, misinterpretation of what teachers say, false accusations of teachers, frequent complaints of unfair treatment, complaints that teachers or parents "have it in for" him or her, extreme suspiciousness of teachers' motives, insolence, temper or aggressive outbursts when corrected or requested to do something, resentment of authority, unwillingness to obey rules and regulations, hostile reactions to discipline.

● **Interpersonal Signs: Other Students**
Bullying, teasing, pushiness, trying to be funny, acting tough, dominating and controlling younger or smaller students, showing off, abusive or obscene language, frequent verbal and physical 'fights' with peers, regular complaints that other students do not like him or her, frequent relaying of 'dirty' stories, over-interest in sexual matters.

C. Signs of Over-Control
● **Personal Signs: Student**
Extreme shyness, poor or no self-confidence, strong tendency to remain alone, homesickness, school 'phobia', highly insecure and anxious, timidity, fearfulness of new situations, mutism, avoidance of school games, tendency to stay apart at break times, over-

academic efforts, frequent daydreaming, worries unduly, frequently looks sad, poor motivation to learn, appears 'lost in another world', obsessional and/or compulsive behaviours, over-exact, meticulous, undue anxiety over performance and undue distress over mistakes and failures, preoccupation with scholastic results, 'perfect' student.

● **Interpersonal Signs: Teacher**

Poor response to recognition and praise, irrelevant answers to questions, failure to respond when addressed, poor or no spontaneous participation in class, over-attachment to one teacher, little or no contact with teachers, no requests for help, hypersensitive to criticism, feelings easily hurt, no eye-contact, extreme nervousness when answering questions, frequent breaking off of speech in the middle of a sentence, frequent mental blocks when either answering questions or doing an examination.

● **Interpersonal Signs: Other Students**

No friends, overt rejection by peers, avoidance of students of opposite sex, absence from school events, avoidance of team games, frequent target of fun by other students.

It is clear from the above outline of student distress that the conflict of each student is peculiar to his or her home and school circumstances and has to be understood and responded to within those special contexts. Nevertheless, we know that all children or adolescents who manifest problems within school inevitably have self-esteem problems which are directly and closely related to their inner conflicts (level 3). Research has also shown that many learning difficulties are related to low self-esteem and the primary target of remedial teachers needs to be the elevation of the child's self-esteem. When the latter is accomplished the child becomes motivated and open to academic input. It has already been pointed out that teachers who establish close affirming relationships with pupils are the most effective teachers. Why so? Affirming relationships of their very nature elevate the self-esteem of students. One of the primary means of raising students' self-esteem is through the relationship that teachers have with students in the classroom. The type of relationship will determine whether or not self-esteem is positively affected. Whether teachers are aware of it or not a student's self esteem is constantly being affected by teachers' interactions with him or her.

3. TEACHER-STUDENT RELATIONSHIPS

There are six types of teacher-student relationships that can operate within a school. Primary school children can be fortunate if they have an affirming, positive teacher as they will have him or her for at least a year and sometimes longer. Of course the reverse is also true - primary school children can be stuck with a strict, critical, negative, punishing teacher for a considerable length of time. Matters are much more confusing for second level pupils because in any one day they can experience a range of different types of relationships with the different teachers they encounter. Five of the six types of relationships described below damage self-esteem.

a. Absence of Relationship

In this classroom a student may be totally ignored or dismissed by a teacher. Nothing that the student does will gain him or her recognition or approval from the teacher. It is literally a 'no win' situation. A student in this classroom who has middle to low self-esteem will be seriously adversely affected by this teacher. A student with high self-esteem will also be minimally affected but generally will get support and help from home to withstand the negative effects of this relationship. The teacher who operates in this non-relating way has serious, deep-seated, self-esteem difficulties and needs professional help.

b. Relationship Devoid of Feelings

This teacher-student relationship is purely clinical or instrumental in nature. The teacher shows no warmth or closeness to students. (S)he is there to teach and not to relate. As in the last type of relationship this is a 'no-win' situation, There is nothing that the student can do to gain approval or acceptance from this teacher. Very often this teacher is seen as a 'good' teacher as (s)he will prepare his/her classes well and deliver effectively academic material within the classroom. However, his or her action will have no elevating effect on self-esteem and for those students with middle to low self-esteem, the teacher's 'cold' relating can have a devastating effect. This teacher also has an enormous self-esteem problem.

c. Narcissistic Relationship

The narcissistic teacher-student relationship is a conditional relationship wherein the pupil can gain recognition and affirmation but at a cost. In effect, the teacher is saying to the student "you are there for me". In this relationship the student is there to meet the teacher's needs and when (s)he does so (s)he will gain praise and approval. This teacher is dependent on his or her own professional performance as a means of gaining approval from others and acceptance of self. Once the students measure up to this teacher's standards they will be affirmed and praised. However, if they fall short they are then likely to be dismissed, ignored, criticised, compared to the students who are measuring up, ridiculed and scolded. All of the latter damage students' self-esteem and perpetuate the dependency and self-esteem difficulties of the teacher. The sad thing is that the children who 'fall short' of the teacher's unrealistic demands are those who will already have middle to low levels of self-esteem. The exposure to such a narcissistic relationship will further lower their feelings about themselves. It is important to see that most parents and teachers are narcissistic in behaviour to some degree or other. This is manifested in the conditional way that most children (and we were all children) are reared. As we have already seen typical conditions that operate in many homes and classrooms are: be good, behave, be clever, be like me, be quick, don't ask questions, be perfect, be like your mother/sister, be athletic. The withdrawal of affection and affirmation from children breaking these conditions is what leads to self-esteem difficulties. Behaviour now becomes the measure of the child's worth and love is the weapon used to shape the child's development.

d. Over-Involved Relationship

This is also a conditional relationship but opposite in nature to narcissistic relating. The basis for this type of relationship is actually the same as for the one just discussed, namely the need for acceptance and approval arising from a teacher's poor level of self-esteem. This teacher is the 'people-pleaser'. (S)he will go to extremes in order to be 'needed' by students and colleagues. This teacher will feel that (s)he 'cannot be done without' and will work long hours and take on extra-curricular activities as a means of developing this indispensability. Remember these actions are subconsciously motivated and any confrontation on their 'martyrdom' nature will evoke such defensive responses as "My job is all important to me" or "People need me" and so on. Compared to narcissistic relationships this over-involved interacting says "I am there for you" and "As long as you let me do things for you and be a part of your life, I will accept and value you". The real, but hidden, issue is " I can't live without someone needing or approving of me". The condition for acceptance is quite clear "need me". Students who do not respond to this condition and who want to be independent in decision-making and in ways of doing things and who generally want to be separate and not over-protected will be rejected by this teacher, mainly in the form of withdrawal, silence and even sulking.

Clearly, both of the last two types of relating mask similar self-esteem problems except that narcissistic relating employs dominance and control to gain recognition and over-involved relating uses 'people-pleasing' as the medium to gain recognition. Either way the student loses out if (s)he does not respond. But even if (s)he does meet the conditions (s)he still loses out on two accounts. One, (s)he develops a dependency on the teacher for approval and, two, (s)he sacrifices his or her own identity formation and independence in order to please either of these two types of teachers.

e. Symbiotic Relationships

This is a very disturbing relationship wherein no individuality is allowed and each member of the class (or family) must be the same in all aspects of behaviour. It is as if the class (or family) is the individual and the members make up that one body. This used to be very common in monasteries and convents. I spent seven years in a semi-enclosed order myself and during those years we had to dress the same, have the same philosophical and theological ideas, walk the same, eat the same food and so on. Individuality and independence were anathema to this system. Any attempt to be different was severely punished. Some classrooms and staffrooms can be symbiotic wherein the teacher or principal demands this sameness and absolute inter-dependency. Because this style of relating attempts to totally block identity development and independence, which are the bases of high self-esteem, it is extremely damaging and its effects are as great as for a. and b. above.

All of the above five ways of relating increase insecurity and lack of confidence and lower self-esteem in children. Each student needs the teacher/student relationship to demonstrate that his or her **presence** is valuable and worthwhile within each class and within the school. It is equally important that a student's **absence** matters and that this is communicated to him or her. Many teachers 'breathe a sigh of relief' when a particular pupil is absent and when that student returns the non-verbal language will be one that reveals "oh no, (s)he's back!". Children are excellent at reading non-verbal behaviour and when this is negative their sense of value is again undermined. It is necessary then that the student feels that both his or her presence and absence matters.

f. Empathic Relationship

Fortunately, there is a healthy, self-esteem building way for teachers to interact with students. This type of relationship is of an unconditional nature wherein each student is valued and affirmed for his or her unique person and being. Students' differences in size, shape, colour, social background, level of knowledge, academic or athletic skills are respected and appreciated. Teachers show interest in each student because they value and respect him or her as a unique human being deserving of affirmation. In this unconditional interaction the valuing relationship is seen as the priority and is never broken because of unacceptable behaviours, mistakes or failures. The affirmative teacher is just as strict as the conditional, rigid and authoritarian teacher when it comes to children learning to take responsibility for their actions. But this firmness is executed always within the context of the warm and affirming relationship. Furthermore, the child is not 'put down' but is helped to become aware of the necessity to learn responsibility and if (s)he attempts to slide out of responsibility then the teacher has no choice but to impose consequences (more about this in next chapter). Criticism, scoldings, 'put-down' messages, ridicule, comparing students, sarcasm, cynicism are absent in this teacher-student relationship. Futhermore, the child is encouraged to express in constructive ways his or her opinions and any worries, fears, grievances, resentments, frustration, difficulties (s)he may be experiencing. At all times the child knows that (s)he is accepted for his or her person and that behaviour is not the yardstick to measure worth.

4. STUDENT SELF-ESTEEM IN THE CLASSROOM

The section on maladaptive behaviour has indicated that the hidden conflicts of children presenting problems within the classroom are virtually always related to self-esteem. It is then in the interest of the class teacher and all other teachers in the school to find ways of elevating the feelings and attitudes these students possess about themselves. Elevation of student self-esteem will considerably decrease the amount and intensity of classroom problems.

A. Identifying Students with Low Self-Esteem

Identifying the student with poor self-esteem is not difficult and the short checklist below will help towards this end.

Checklist for Low Self-Esteem in Students

a.   *Over-control indicators: student may be:*
- Shy and withdrawn
- Reluctant to take on new activities/challenges
- Unable to easily mix with other students
- Over-conscientious or apathetic in learning situations
- Fearful and timid in new situations
- Easily upset if corrected
- Daydreamer
- Fearful of failures and mistakes
- In the habit of putting self down

b. *Under-control indicators: student may be:*
- Boastful
- Regular truant
- Frequent requester of help or reassurance
- Attention seeking
- Continually asking if (s)he is liked or popular
- Avoider of work even though risking teacher's disap-proval
- Blaming of others for his/her mistakes or failures
- Prone to regular aggressive outbursts

B. Self-Esteem and Learning

Many teachers are often puzzled by students who clearly possess the skills to learn but make no effort in that direction. The high self-esteem child will have retained a natural curiosity for learning and will be enthusiastic when presented with a new challenge. This child is confident in social situations and in tackling academic assignments. Somehow the middle/low self-esteem child has lost that excitement of learning; indeed any learning means risking failure and mistakes and these have only brought humiliation and rejection in the past. It is safer to risk teacher's disapproval rather than the embarrassment and punishment of failure.

The interesting thing about children and learning is that success and failure in themselves have no effect on their drive to learn but the reactions of parents, teachers and other significant adults to success and failure can have a devastating effect on a child's motivation to learn. When parents, teachers and others react positively to successful performances and punishingly (eg. shouting, blaming, ridicule, scoldings etc.) to failure, the child will now begin to doubt his or her ability to please significant adults in his or her life and his or her capability of doing what is requested. This child has to find ways of protecting himself or herself from such harsh conditionality. There are, in effect, two choices open to him or her: **Avoidance** or **Compensation**. Both of these sub-conscious reactions are survival strategies for living in a painful world of conditionality. The more extreme are the reactions of significant adults the more intense and enduring are the child's protective behaviours. **Avoidance** of scholastic demands is such a clever strategy because it means that with no effort there can be no failure and no failure means no humiliation.

Unfortunately, a teacher may often become frustrated, annoyed and angry with this student and blame, ridicule or scold, which will drive the child further into the conviction that (s)he is worthless in the eyes of adults. Avoidance behaviour will increase in spite of the punishment meted out.

The second survival strategy is **compensation** and here the child either fights back at the source of frustration or (s)he tries extremely hard to please both parents and teachers. The latter is very often seen as virtuous by adults but teachers need to be vigilant in noticing this child because failure and mistakes or even a small drop in standard of performance can be a devastating blow to this child's sense of self.

It is often this student who is a suicide risk or who can experience severe anxiety and panic attacks coming up to examination time. Sometimes these students may be hospitalised and have often been misclassified as suffering from 'schizophrenia'. It reminds me of an A-level student in England who was referred to me for psychotherapy. She had been one of the best students the school ever had. She was extremely attentive in class, no absenteeism, conscientious in completing home-work assignments, A-level performance in all subjects - a perfect student! When she went into her A-level year in September the teachers began to notice a radical change in her classroom behaviour. For the first time she was clearly not listening and she began to fail to complete assignments. They also noticed that she seemed quite distressed; this manifesting itself in facial grimacing. At home she spent all her time locked away in her bedroom. She was unwilling to talk to anyone about what was disturbing her. Finally, after three weeks her mother persuaded her to reveal her conflict. The girl was terrified because she felt, in her own words, that she was "possessed by the devil". She was brought to a psychiatrist who labelled her 'schizophrenic' and had her hospitalised and put on medication. Her parents were dissatisfied with her progress and had heard from a teacher within the school that I worked in a non-organic way with people labelled 'schizophrenic'. On discharge from hospital, the girl came to see me with her parents. The school had already contacted me and I had developed some insights into her ways of behaving and the high academic performance pressures on the girl from teachers, parents and herself. The school principal had outlined her 'brilliant' academic record and the fact that the girl was a very quiet and reserved person never giving any trouble at all. When I went to my waiting room she was sitting between her parents, clearly still in a highly stressed state. All her features were distorted, her head was bowed and her body twisting as in agony. I was worried that she might be too disassociated from reality and not be able to respond to my helping efforts. I invited her on her own over to my office. I had already asked myself the question "why now?". This girl seemed to have coped well up to the September of this year but had suffered a radical change in behaviour since returning to school. Clearly, being her last year in secondary school, her A-levels year, the pressure on her to perform would be greater than it ever had been before. So the difference was that this was her A-levels year. The fact too that this girl bottled-up all her feelings and problems meant that her conflict would not reveal itself through conscious behaviours (what I say, think and feel) but through unconscious means. The language of the unconscious is metaphorical and, in my experience, delusions and hallucinations are messages regarding hidden conflicts. It is readily acceptable that dreams reveal conflicts that need resolution in our lives. Hallucinations and delusions are like 'waking dreams'; an attempt by the psyche to wake a person up to intrapsychic and extrapsychic issues that need to be changed in his or her life. This girl had literally interpreted her feeling of being possessed by the devil and her reaction was one of terror that she was going insane. The psychiatrist interpreted that delusion as an organic dysfunction. When you see the delusion as meaningful, the sense of it begins to emerge. I knew this young person had attained a high level of knowledge and, if she was hearing me, she would begin to get insight into her crisis experience. I explained to her how the mind reveals conflicts in different ways, through aggression, withdrawal, hostility, negative thinking, dependency, fears and metaphor. I explained that I felt that her 'being possessed by the devil' was a clear message to her of the intense pressure she had been undergoing in this all important examination year. I said that "it seems to me that you have 'a devil of a pressure' inside you, and that also, since the beginning of September you have 'gone to the devil' in not being attentive in class and completing assignments. "Furthermore", I explained, "it would appear to me that all these people that have being putting pressure on you for high scholastic performance, that you would want to say to them 'go to the devil'. As I outlined my hypotheses to this girl, the facial grimacing and body twisting began to ease down and at the end of the session she was quiet and relaxed. She now had meaning for her so called 'insane' experiences. I brought her parents in and explained to them what I felt was the problem. The father was quick to see my explanation and wisely responded by saying "we're the ones that need the therapy". He recognised the immense pressure they had been putting on their daughter. I asked both parents to go to the sidelines of their daughter's life and have no more talk about examinations and academic performance. I also contacted the school and asked teachers not to put pressure on the girl. The three of them, daughter and parents, came for therapy sessions over the following six months. The girl returned to school the day after her first session and the school reported an eighty per cent improvement in the first week. Following two more therapeutic sessions there was one hundred per cent return to attentiveness and completion of assignments. The following summer the girl attained remarkably high A-level results and is now attending University. However, the over compensation strategy no longer is operating as she no longer feels she has to prove herself to her parents, others and self and feels she can enjoy learning for learning's sake.

The child then who tries too hard, who has an over-emphasis on school-work and neglects social, emotional, creative, athletic and leisure activities, has low self-esteem and is attempting to compensate for this inner insecurity by 'being the best' student. The rationale is "If I'm the best, will you now love me Mum, Dad and teacher?".

The other type of compensation is revealed in boastful, aggressive, 'chip on the shoulder' type behaviour. This is the student who rebels against those who impose high and unrealistic demands on him or her. The pose of this student is "I can do anything if I put my mind to it, but why should I please you, why should I bother?". The sad thing is that it bothers him or her greatly that (s)he is not valued but (s)he is not going to show that vulnerability to anyone. This student has developed yet another clever strategy to avoid failure and humiliation. His or her rebelliousness means (s)he avoids having to apply himself or herself to academic demands and therefore (s)he now avoids any risk of failure. If you attempt to coerce such students into applying themselves to their studies they will resist all the more and may act out quite violently. By pushing them you are getting too close to their vulnerability, their fear of failure and rejection, and they now have to defend themselves more fiercely.

It can be seen that all three types of defence strategies employed by students with low self-esteem, have the common element of an attempt to avoid failure and humiliation. The over-intense student avoids failure through high work-input, the student who is arrogant and boastful avoids failure through non-compliance, and the student who is withdrawn and apathetic avoids failure through absence of effort. Why? The answer is that there is a **prime** need in our culture for **self-regard**: a need to be liked and valued.

An important rule for both parents and teachers to be aware of is that **unrealistic** demands lead to low self-esteem but equally **no demands** at all lead to low self-esteem (as no belief is shown in the child's capability). In both cases children are doomed to low achievement or over achievement. The parent and teacher who are effective know that there must be an optimum of pressure - just enough to cause the child to feel challenged and positive but not so much that (s)he becomes distressed. The secret is to be aware of the child's present level of functioning and to work out from there in a **realistic** manner.

Without attention to self-esteem students are not likely to make long-term academic progress. Research is showing that, in general, people's levels of achievement are influenced by how they see themselves and, more specifically, that self-esteem and scholastic achievement are strongly associated. A teacher in the classroom is in a powerful position to influence how students feel about themselves. The most important vehicle the teacher has is the relationship with the student and when this is valuing and caring in nature students' self-esteem will be elevated.

Teaching then is more effective when teachers concentrate on the development of scholastic abilities and on the student's affective state and on self-esteem in particular. Education is not just about developing intellectual and occupational skills, it is also about helping students to understand and value themselves, to be able to communicate in effective ways with others, to appreciate and celebrate all aspects of life, to develop healthy relationships with others and their world, to be able to cope with the physical, emotional and social difficulties of life, to become self-motivated and self-directed.

C. Increasing Self-Esteem in the Classroom

Each student in a classroom has a particular level of self-esteem. As in the case of teachers the child's level of self-esteem will largely determine how that child behaves in the classroom. By the time a child arrives into the primary school his or her home experiences will already have determined how (s)he feels about himself or herself. How parents and other significant adults in the child's life respond to the child determines how the child will view himself or herself. Parental responses to the child are the looking glass through which the child evaluates himself or herself in terms of his or her lovability and capability. If the child is rarely physically held, frequently scolded, ridiculed, criticised, compared, physically abused, has unfair expectations put on him or her, then (s)he will be convinced of unworthiness. Within the family a child's awareness of his or her psychological, social and physical characteristics emerges through his or her family experiences of either being loved/not loved and being seen as capable/not capable or clever/ stupid etc. Within the school and classroom a child's evaluation of self emerges through the school and classroom experiences of being popular/unpopular and capable/not capable. For a teacher to raise students' self-esteem it is necessary that (s)he first elevates his/her own feelings about self. Research shows that the teacher with high self-esteem automatically produces students with high self-esteem but the converse is also sadly true. It is important for teachers to be aware that every word, every facial expression, gesture or action on the part of the teacher gives the student some message about his or her worth.

The teacher needs to ensure that all actions towards students are of a nature that raises self-esteem. This takes considerable awareness and effort but the consequences are highly rewarding in terms of positive school and classroom environments. Elevating students' self-esteem does not take any extra class time. Indeed, it is the students with low self-esteem who take up a great amount of class time. Elevating these students' self-esteem will reduce the class disruption they cause and so make for more teaching time. Also, surely the emotional well-being of the student is as important as his or her academic development. In any case if the child has emotional difficulties, (s)he is less likely to make academic progress or, as you have seen, may put immense strain on himself/ herself to achieve, unless these emotional issues are resolved.

The absence of behaviours in the classroom that damage self-esteem is paramount. These include criticism, sarcasm, cynicism, comparison of students , ridicule, scoldings, 'put-down' messages, physical abuse, taunting, negative labelling and ignoring students so that they feel invisible in your classroom. Students, like teachers, have an immense need to be liked, valued and visible. When this does not occur they will sub-consciously find ways of being seen in your classroom, either through withdrawal or aggressive/disruptive behaviours. One of my recommendations to teachers is to ensure that as children file into the classroom and during class time, you make either some non-verbal or verbal contact with each student, thus establishing their visibility within the classroom. Such contact can be in the form of eye contact, a greeting, a smile, a nod, a 'welcome back' for a student who was absent, a word of concern for a child who has had, for example, a bereavement in the family or a hospitalised parent, a pat on the shoulder - anything that lets students know that they are positively seen by you. Maintain that type of contact throughout the day.

Apart from the absence of negative behaviours and the presence of contact responses, there are certain powerful messages that teachers can communicate to students that will raise their level of self-esteem. Clearly, the child with low self-esteem needs to experience these messages much more frequently than the middle to high self-esteem student. These messages are:

- "You're behaviour is always right"
- "You belong"
- "You can make sense and order out of your world"
- "You are capable in what you do and you please me"
- "You are one of a kind and special"
- "You have a right to your own unique growing"

We have already considered the first message and recognised that maladaptive behaviour is a psychological sign of underlying self-esteem problems and that it is expedient for the teacher, with the help of the Principal and colleagues, to uncover those hidden issues that are causing this student to slide out of mature development and responsibility. It has also been shown that though the maladaptive behaviours may be saying something 'right' about the student, they can be socially unacceptable to the teacher and other students and that some constructive responses are needed to curtail the disruption they cause (see Chapter Five). Nonetheless, when students see that teachers are understanding and compassionate, though positively firm, they are much more likely to respond to the needs of the teacher for responsible behaviours in the classroom. However, if the student feels 'put down' by the teacher, problems are much more likely to escalate.

The second message of 'you belong' that elevates self-esteem has been considered under teacher-student relationships (section 3 of this chapter). Here each student needs to tangibly see that (s)he makes a difference, that his or her **presence** and **absence** matter to the teacher and to the school as a whole. The relationship must be such that the student knows without question that (s)he is an important member of the class and school and is automatically included among 'us' in any formulation of 'us' and 'them'. Belonging is also communicated through photographs and work of students being displayed on classroom walls and school corridors.

Security for children develops from experiencing a world that is generally consistent and predictable in meeting their needs. This is an ever-ending process as the needs of children, adolescents and adults keep multiplying. When needs are only met now and again or rarely, the child will now begin to experience the world (home, classroom, school) as unpredictable and unsafe. (S)he will also conclude that it is something within him or her that has led to being neglected. On the other hand, when children's needs are fairly consistently met, the world becomes predictable, or at least understandable, and they will conclude that they are basically worthy. The needs of children are many: physical, emotional, intellectual, social, sensual, recreational, spiritual, behavioural, imaginative and creative. Within these need areas they have other needs, the needs to be challenged, to have more and more freedom as they grow older, to be protected, to have limits, to be responsible, to receive advice and counsel and to experience a sense of humour. Predictability and consistency are the hallmarks of effective classroom management as children know precisely how this teacher responds to both responsible and irresponsible behaviours. Students also know within this classroom that their needs to be valued, encouraged, recognised and positively corrected will be consistently met. In this way then the child learns that (s)he can make sense and order of the worlds of classroom and school.

The medium of behaviour is the primary means that children use to impress adults and to be competent. It is important to realise that a child's behaviour has two goals: to establish competence in what (s)he does and to develop competence in relationships. Indeed, this ability to elicit expressions of approval and acceptance from parent figures in the child's life will be tested over and over again. Later, this need to impress others extends beyond the immediate family, to teachers, fellow students, relatives and so on. It is not then sufficient for a teacher to notice a child's competency. The teacher must also show obvious approval and acceptance. If that does not happen the child may develop high competence in what (s)he does but (s)he will have no confidence that his or her behaviour is of any value. Teachers then need to respond at a double level to a student's efforts - recognising the effort and showing they are impressed by same. I deliberately use the term 'effort' as most parents and teachers tend to respond to performance which leads to all sorts of activity and motivational problems for children. **Every effort is an attainment** and can be shaped-up to higher levels of competency. If an effort is criticised because of performance standard then children will either stop trying, or become tentative about risk-taking (common phenomenon also among adults!) or over-try. For example, Michael, aged 3 years, is very proud. He has managed to put on his own shoes for the first time all by himself. "Look Mommy", he announces, proudly, looking down at his shoes. Mother responds critically, "you put them on the wrong feet". Mother has totally missed what Michael has attained and now makes it more unlikely he will try again.

A similar approach is needed when children's class or home-work is being corrected. The emphasis needs to be on the child's effort and the competence level of that effort is where the child is at. Every teacher with experience knows that you can only work out from where the child is at, so any 'mistakes' or 'failures' are only indices of the need for persistent effort on the child's part so that his or her competency will continue to increase. Mistakes and failures are not indicative of capability (which is vast) but only of present level of knowledge. However, teachers and lecturers tend to mark academic work on performance rather than on effort. Let us take a simple example of feedback to a child given five spellings to write out and then to present for examination by the teacher. The teacher gets back the following from the child.

Word Given	Child's Response
(Boat)	Bote
(Seat)	Seet
(Look)	Look
(Coat)	Cote
(Rain)	Rane

The feedback to the child needs to focus on effort, on where the child is at in terms of competency and what further efforts are needed to bring about an increase in competency. What typically happens is that the child would get back the following:

Bote   ✗   Cote   ✗
Seet   ✗   Rane   ✗
Look   ✔

The above can be devastating to children as it highlights what knowledge they have not got rather than what they have attained. The appropriate feedback is first to always give a mark for the effort of doing the spellings and then highlight what has been attained, as follows:

✔   (effort Mark)
Bote
✔
Seet   *Here the letters that*
✔   *were correctly placed*
Look   ✔   *or paired are*
Cote   *highlighted.*
✔
Rane
✔

The above now reinforces the child for efforts and attainment level and points out to the teacher where the child's next efforts need to be directed; from the starting point of where (s)he is presently at.

The same principles apply when giving feedback to students at University. Highlight what they have attained and give written or verbal suggestions of where their next effort needs to go. It needs to be pointed out strongly that grades are not measures of their capability but only of their present level of knowledge. Let them know that efforts in the directions suggested will reap the reward of more knowledge.

These principles also apply to the situation of asking questions of children in the classroom. When a student does not know or only partially knows the answer to your question regarding a particular piece of knowledge, the student is then ripe for learning. However, if you now pass onto the next student, or even worse still, make some sarcastic remark, you have now undermined the first student's self-esteem.

It is wise to direct or help the first student to attain to the knowledge level (s)he clearly has not yet reached. In doing that you will not damage your relationship with the student and (s)he is more likely to remain motivated to learn. The next question you ask the class must be **different** from the previous question as otherwise you will be 'showing-up' the first student's present lack of knowledge.

Another important principle in educating others is to ensure that **learning always has positive associations.** Parents need very much to be included in this direction, as too often home lessons are battlegrounds wherein parents scold, shout, roar, show obvious disapproval or make comparisons. Many teachers still give 'lines' or extra school-work as a punishment for misbehaviour and then they wonder why children 'hate' school. The more children experience positive responses to their learning efforts the more likely it is they will retain their natural curiosity for knowledge and remain highly motivated to learn.

The fifth message the child needs to receive from parents and teachers concerns his or her social self. A person's social self is largely concerned with the sense of being different, separate and unique. No two people are the same. A child's self-esteem requires that (s)he be comfortable and accepting of his or her specialness. Most adults do not have that kind of acceptance; the reason being that as children parents, teachers and others did not celebrate and encourage optimisation of their uniqueness. Difference is not a characteristic that is highly valued in homes and classrooms. A child needs to see clearly that (s)he is accepted and valued for his or her unique self. Teachers communicate that vital message that "you are one of a kind and special" by letting the child know that there is room in the relationship for him or her to be different in values, perception, feelings and physical attributes (size, shape, colour). Teachers need also encourage the child to learn at his or her own pace. In exercising separation and difference the child needs to know that (s)he does not jeopardise his or her place in the classroom or school.

The sixth message is concerned with helping children find their own unique life pattern. Teachers and parents who dominate and control prevent the development of this process and so damage self-esteem. The 'mother's vocation' was a reality for many people who went into a religious career in this country. This also happens within other professions. I remember helping one young man who had been rejected by his parents (both medical doctors) because he would not go on to do medicine. When he came to see me he had 'dropped out' of college, was feeling really guilty about letting his parents down and was at a loss as to what he should do about his career development. Many misguided parents want their children to have the opportunities and accomplishments they did not have. The problem is that they forget to ask the child about what (s)he wants. Also times change and, most of all, the child is not a photocopy of the parent. It would help children enormously if teachers would encourage them to pursue what 'fits' for them and not live other people's lives through responding to parents and teachers' projections of their own needs. The child who is pursuing his or her own unique path retains high motivation for learning and the converse is also true. Even if a child acquiesces to parents' or teachers' projections there will always be a hidden resentment and a feeling of non-self-fulfillment.

There are other actions on the part of the teacher that can aid the development of self-esteem in the classroom:

- **Genuineness and sincerity on the part of the teacher**
- **Personal time with students**
- **Delegation of routine jobs**
- **Making requests rather than commanding**
- **Positive non-verbal and verbal behaviour**

Being genuine means being a 'real' person and not hiding behind a 'professional mask' or manner. It means being honest, open and spontaneous and being separate in communicating with students. The latter is essential as a student's behaviour is always a revelation about him or her and not a message about you as the teacher. If you fail to remain separate it means you become defensive and inevitable conflict between you and the student ensues. This conflict undermines the child's self-esteem. The teacher who is 'real' also has the ability to recognise success and failure as relative terms and not as absolute measures of children's worth. Being genuine demands that teachers are honest in their appraisal of themselves and do not project their conflict issues onto students.

Personal time with students was alluded to at the beginning of this section. The principle issue here is that the closer the relationship with the student the more it enhances that student's self-esteem. The student with low self-esteem needs far more personal contact than the middle to high self-esteem child. This personal time is not meant to be of an invasive nature but one where interest, concern and affection is shown towards an individual child. All the indicators are that when a student perceives a teachers as liking him or her, (s)he will not abuse that relationship in any setting, whether within or outside the school.

There are always odd jobs that a teacher needs doing and these provide the opportunity to enhance a particular student's self-esteem. It is best to give these jobs to the pupils with low self-esteem as they are in need of ways to impress teachers. Generally speaking, teachers tend to give such jobs to the 'more able' student who is not in need of urgent self-esteem enhancement.

When we request we show respect to the student's right to freedom of response and we are egalitarian in communicating. When we command, control and dominate we lower self-esteem.

Finally, teachers need to guard against non-verbal and verbal communication that is detrimental to self-esteem development. As has been pointed out, children are quite sensitive to non-verbal cues from others, these cues can communicate messages along the dimensions of likes/dislikes, interested/not interested and superior/inferior. Examples of such cues are body posture, eye contact, body orientation, tone of voice, pauses in speech, speed of speech, facial expression and gestures. Verbal messages are more obvious and it can be more clearly seen how they can enhance or reduce self-esteem. Again, it is essential that they are of a positive nature such as encouraging, affirming, praising, valuing and calming. Be sure that the verbal message is congruent with your non-verbal communication. If there is incongruence, if there is a discrepancy between the two levels, the child will nearly always relate to the non-verbal message.

5. KEY ISSUES

- Students' maladaptive behaviours are indicators of 'hidden' conflict issues unique to each child.

- Students' maladaptive behaviours are signs which should not be allowed to be shown in vain.

- A student's problematic behaviour is called 'maladaptive' because it never resolves the hidden conflict issue.

- It is not difficult for teachers to identify the at risk student.

- Students' maladaptive responses can be usefully categorised as under-control and over-control behaviours.

- Some maladaptive behaviours, though psychologically 'right' are socially unacceptable.

- Students' self-esteem in the classroom is largely determined by the type of teacher-student relationship.

- The only relationship that enhances students' self-esteem is an empathic, unconditional one.

- There is a high correlation between level of students' self-esteem and motivation to learn and academic attainment.

- Students with middle to low self-esteem may use **avoidance** or **compensation** to avoid the humiliation of failure.

- Constructive and **realistic** challenges are needed for children to develop a sense of capability.

- Without attention to self-esteem students with learning difficulties are unlikely to make long-term progress.

- All actions of the teacher towards the student communicate a message about the child's worth and this happens whether the teacher is aware or not of this process.

- Every academic effort is an attainment.

- Mistakes and failures are opportunities for learning.

- Comparison of one student with another is an act of rejection of the student compared and it also puts pressure on the 'model' student to be always 'one-up'.

- Learning must always have positive associations.

- There are certain teacher behaviours towards students that enhance self-esteem and others that reduce it.

6. KEY TASKS

- Discover the hidden conflict(s) of students manifesting either under-control or over-control maladaptive behaviours.

- Early identification of the at-risk student will prevent escalation of maladaptive behaviours.

- Be aware of creating a destructive type of relationship with students in the classroom as it will only generate self-esteem problems in students.

- Create an empathic and unconditional relationship with each student in the classroom.

- Do not break the relationship with the student because of a maladaptive behaviour on his or her part.

- Positively and firmly correct the maladaptive behaviour but **not** the person of the student.

- The student who avoids or is over-involved or hostile to academic effort and demands is masking a self-esteem problem and needs your help.

- Put the emphasis on responding to academic effort rather than academic performance.

- Be sure there is not too wide a gap between your academic expectations and the student's present level of attainment.

- Employ mistakes and failures as opportunities for teaching **not** criticising.

- Attendance to students' self-esteem will lead to greater academic effort.

- Avoid the use of criticism, ridiculing, scolding, 'put-down' messages, sarcasm and cynicism as these only damage students' self-esteem and lead to problems in the classroom.

- Find ways to make each student visible in your classroom.

- Send verbal and non-verbal messages that elevate students' self-esteem.

- It is important that the student knows from you that both his or her **presence** and **absence** matter.

- Be **predictable** and **consistent** in the way you respond to students.

- Correct students' work in a way that emphasises effort, present level of attainment and indicate where the next academic effort needs to be directed.

- Do not ask another student the same question that you have asked of a student who did not know the answer.

- Personal time with students enhances their self-esteem.

- The student with low self-esteem needs more centering by means of personal time with you, delegation of routine jobs and frequent affirmation.

CHAPTER FIVE

The Classroom

1. CLASSROOM CONTROL IS NOT THE TEACHER'S RESPONSIBILITY

2. PROBLEMS OF OVER-CONTROL AND UNDER-CONTROL

3. UNDER-CONTROL PROBLEMS IN CLASSROOMS

4. MALADAPTIVE BEHAVIOURS OF TEACHERS WITHIN CLASSROOMS

   - Checklist

5. ESSENTIAL ASPECTS OF CLASSROOM MANAGEMENT

   - Checklist of positive in-class teacher behaviours

6. DESIGNING A SYSTEM OF STUDENT RESPONSIBILITY

   - In-class and out-of-class student responsibilities
   - Positive use of sanctions
   - List of available sanctions

7. IMPLEMENTATION OF A STUDENT RESPONSIBILITY SYSTEM

8. RESPONDING TO A STUDENT WHO IS RECALCITRANT

- ABC analysis of maladaptive behaviour

9. USE OF BACK-UP PROFESSIONAL SERVICES

- When to refer a student for specialised help

10. KEY ISSUES

11. KEY TASKS

1. CLASSROOM CONTROL IS NOT THE TEACHER'S RESPONSIBILITY

It is not the teacher's job to control children in the classroom! This goes contrary to what I learned and practised as a teacher. However, closer examination of traditional discipline practises reveals that it is a recipe for conflict to get one person to control another. You know that as an adult when a person attempts to control you or gives unsolicited advice you react defensively. The same holds for children and adolescents. Effective classroom management is based on the principle that each member of the class, student and teacher, is responsible for his or her own self-control. It is not then the job of the teacher to control children but it is the responsibility of children to control themselves. Equally the teacher has the responsibility to be in control of himself or herself and any loss of control with children is an abrogation of that responsibility. Indeed, if a teacher frequently loses control (s)he is hardly in a position to request children to take charge of themselves. Furthermore, this teacher models lack of self-control for students and it is the tendency of children to imitate adults! Yet another issue is that the teacher who responds negatively and aggressively to children is, in fact, giving the children control over him or her. In this classroom the children know they can 'get under the skin' of the teacher and as children generally are not given a lot of power in classrooms this bit of power becomes a weapon to be used, particularly when children's self-esteem is under threat.

Good classroom management is aimed at **educating children to take responsibility for themselves.** In any social system the members have certain responsibilities so that order, safety, fairness, justice and harmony are promoted. For example, there are certain responsibilities motor road users have so that road systems are effectively utilised. When you are caught for speeding in a thirty-mile zone, or for illegal parking, blaming the policeman or traffic warden is hardly fair as you are the one who chose to engage in the act of irresponsibility. The sanctions are there to ensure responsibility. You chose the risk of sanction when you acted irresponsibly. Most people have been very pleased with the strong sanctions that are now in vogue for drunken driving. The person who loses his or her driving licence due to that irresponsibility has chosen that sanction; it is only a further act of irresponsibility to blame the policeman for the imposed sanction.

A school and a classroom are social systems. Within these systems the responsibilities to develop functionality must be clearly spelt out. There are different responsibilities for the different members of the systems: the principal, the vice-principal, teachers with A or B posts, teachers with responsibilities for particular groups of children, the class teacher, the students, the secretaries and others involved. As regards the students their particular responsibilities within the classroom and outside the classroom need to be typed out and pinned up in every classroom. It is desirable that older children be included in the drawing up and the reviewing of such a list.

This list of student responsibilities needs also to clearly specify what sanctions there are when a student fails to meet the agreed responsibility. At the start of the school year and the beginning of every term, the teacher needs to remind the students of those responsibilities and their accompanying sanctions. Most of all (s)he can point out that the choice lies with them, not with the teacher. (S)he will then give the opportunity to voice any objections to the outlined responsibilities and will convey those to the committee responsible for drawing up these responsibilities. At least in second-level schools and upper classes in primary schools, student representatives need to be members of such a committee.

It is wise for teachers to remember that students need frequent reminding of their responsibilities. Also, one of the responsibilities of teachers (like that of a traffic warden) is to **ensure that children do not slide out of responsibility**. This latter needs to come from a position of unconditional valuing of each student and an awareness of the unique potential of each student. When a student chooses to be irresponsible then the teacher justly and fairly imposes the agreed and outlined sanction that the student has chosen to risk when (s)he acted irresponsibly. It is important that the sanction fits the crime as unjust consequences rarely induce responsible behaviour.

Classroom management is largely then the responsibility of students. The teacher's responsibility is to ensure that the devised school and classroom systems are effectively implemented. Frequent reviewing of the effectiveness of any social system is desirable. In this approach the teacher is not seen as the disciplinarian but rather as a presenter of choices and their consequences (both positive and sanctions) and the student is put in clear responsibility of himself or herself. Giving responsibility to students and believing in their ability to meet it are powerful boosts to their self-esteem.

2. PROBLEMS OF OVER-CONTROL AND UNDER-CONTROL

Control difficulties within classrooms have become a major source of stress for many teachers. Old authoritarian methods rarely work anymore and some teachers are left floundering as to how to respond to behavioural problems within the classroom. You have seen that these behavioural difficulties are signs of underlying emotional or social difficulties of children and that attention to these hidden conflicts is essential if long-term resolution is to be achieved. Nevertheless, some direct positive response to the behavioural disruption is needed as learning best takes place in an environment of relative calm and harmony. Earlier a distinction was made between problems of under-control and over-control (Section 1, Chapter 4) and it was indicated that it is the former difficulties that primarily affect classroom management. Most teachers are aware that the student who persistently disrupts the class often has a difficult home background and very often back-up and co-operation from the parents of these students is difficult to acquire. Nonetheless, some knowledge of the possible causes of the student's emotional and behavioural difficulties makes for a better understanding of the problematic behaviour and for a more wide-ranging constructive response to the display of such difficulties.

Emotional and behavioural difficulties in children can arise as a consequence of two types of circumstance which can often coincide.

Firstly, the problems may spring from **shortcomings in the process of socialisation** to which all children are normally exposed. Examples of these are:

- The lack of continuous relationship with mother or mother-substitute or just one adult during the first three years of life.

- Later poor modelling by parents, who do not respect themselves or each other, of socially unacceptable behaviours such as aggression, non-assertiveness, poor communication skills, irresponsibility.

- Absence of essential experiences can also occur when a child is reared in a sub-culture whose values, morals and standards of behaviour differ from those of the larger culture into which the child may have to fit as (s)he grows up.

The second set of circumstances that may lead to emotional and behavioural problems in children is where the child is exposed to **excessive pressure** either from outside or inside himself or himself. The former are the most common and come from dominating, controlling, hypercritical parenting or alcoholism of one or both parents, or marital discord or domestic violence or lack of social ability in either parent or hostility arising from a three-generation family living under the same roof. Difficulties can also arise from 'spoiling' of children as these children do not learn self-control or the ability to tolerate delayed gratification. Inconsistency of positive parenting skills also puts pressure on children as they do not know where the limits are, they can often play one parent off against another and, like adults, they will slide out of responsibilities if they get the chance. Pressure can also arise from within children, such as physical or mental handicap, development delays and poor knowledge levels when they enter school. At least one third of children who have physical and/or mental handicaps also develop emotional difficulties.

3. UNDER-CONTROL PROBLEMS IN CLASSROOMS

The main under-control problems that make it difficult for teachers to conduct their classes are listed below. This is by no means an exhaustive list.

Student's Under-Control Behaviours within Classrooms

(a) **Start of Class**
- Enters room noisily
- Pushes and shoves other students
- Shouts out to others
- Bangs desk on sitting down
- Does not have materials needed for class
- Avoids eye contact
- Ignores teacher's requests

(b) **During Class**
- Tries to be funny
- Turns around in class
- Talks in class
- Rocks in chair
- Walks around classroom
- Talks and mutters to self
- Distracts others
- Lifts desk with knees
- Starts singing
- Makes distracting verbal or physical noises
- Constantly fidgets with apparatus
- Ignores teacher's requests
- Reacts aggressively to feedback
- Does not answer questions addressed to him/her
- Ignores requests for responsibility on his/her part
- Throws paper missiles around class
- Interferes with other pupil's work
- Teases and taunts other students
- Fails to hand-up homework

- Refuses to do classwork
- Has temper outbursts
- Steals other children's possessions
- Makes irrelevant comments
- Damages other students' property
- Absconds from classroom

(c) **End of Class**
- Rushes out of class
- Pushes and shoves others
- Shouts loudly
- Makes 'smart alec' remarks
- Avoids eye-contact
- Ignores teacher's requests for orderly exiting
- Ignores teacher's request to stay behind

(d) **Outside of Class**
- Bullies other students
- Breaks rule of no smoking
- Defaces walls
- Damages school property
- Steals other people's belongings
- Races along school corridors
- Shouts in school corridors

A student who is regularly showing any of the above difficulties needs an immediate, consistent and predictable response. These behavioural manifestations are additional to any learning difficulties (s)he may have and they make this student stand out from his or her peers. Knowing that such students have difficult family situations or a different cultural background is helpful but it is not a reason to say 'nothing can be done'. All the evidence emerging is that a child with emotional, behavioural and cultural differences will adapt into an environment where (s)he is valued, affirmed, respected and positively shaped into accepting responsibility within the classroom and school. It is also a fact that not all children's problems are totally a product of their home situations.

Some problems can be directly traced to the classroom or school situations.The most common of these problems is **fear of the teacher**. Generally speaking teachers of whom children are fearful have a repertoire of behaviours that are of a destructive nature, perhaps the most common being sarcasm, cynicism, irritability, impatience, intolerance and verbal aggressiveness. Sarcasm, cynicism and verbal aggressiveness are unfair weapons that the teacher uses against students whose respect (s)he cannot obtain. All of these behaviours will either precipitate worse manners or withdrawal and silent resentment on the part of the targeted students and they are always emotionally disruptive. The students who are passive get hurt, those who are verbally quick 'talk back' and those who are hostile make scenes. The result is a disruptive classroom environment wherein no one gets much learning done.

Fear of examinations is another problem that arises all too commonly nowadays, within the classroom setting. Its effects are now well known: anxiety, concentration problems, memory difficulties, insomnia, headaches, muscle tension, 'mental blocks', depression, suicidal feelings and so on. This fear comes from too great a pressure for marks by either parents or teacher or both. Teachers would be wise to make academic tests interesting and challenging to students of different levels of ability. They need also to take the pressure off and encourage students to do the best they can. Most of all they need to remind pupils that scholastic performance is no index of their worth as persons.

Finally, some students, particularly in early adolescence, have a **fear of standing up and speaking in class.** This may stem from, for example, sensitivity over their height or voice change and teachers need to be sensitive to this difficulty and attempt to make classwork as informal as possible.

4. MALADAPTIVE BEHAVIOURS OF TEACHERS WITHIN CLASSROOMS

Given that some problems can be traced to factors within the school, it is wise for teachers and principals to look to their own behaviours and see whether these may be a trigger to students' disruptive responses. A list of such behaviours is given below. These maladaptive behaviours on the part of the teacher are indicators of underlying insecurity issues that (s)he needs to own and take responsibility to change.

Teachers' Inappropriate Behaviours within the Classroom
(a)   Teacher-Student Communication
- Shout at Children
- Order, dominate and control children
- Employ cynicism and sarcasm as means of control
- Ridicule, scold, criticise.
- Label students as 'stupid', 'dull', 'weak', 'lazy', etc.
- Physically threaten children
- Push and shove children
- Are violent towards children
- Give schoolwork or 'lines' as punishments
- Do not listen to students
- Compare one student with another
- Are judgemental
- Do not like some students
- Have obvious favourites
- Do not know children's first names
- Do not call students by their first names
- Are too strict
- Are impatient with pupils who are slow in understanding a lesson
- Expect too much of children
- Do not care whether children work or not
- Do not feel any affection for children
- Punish mistakes and failures
- Do not help when the work is difficult
- Never apologise for mistakes
- Do not say 'please' and 'thank you' to students
- Are inconsistent and unpredictable in response to troublesome behaviour

(b) Teachers' Attitudes to Lessons
- Waste time
- Do not make lessons interesting
- Are not prepared for lessons
- Leave class half-way through a lesson
- Pass on to next lesson without regard to students who have not mastered first lesson
- Are programme-centred rather than student-centred

(c) Teachers' Own Emotional State
- Frequently irritable and moody
- Hate teaching
- Doubt own teaching competence
- Fear loss of classroom control
- Worry how colleagues view them
- Want children to like them
- Have low self-esteem
- Fear students

5. ESSENTIAL ASPECTS OF CLASSROOM MANAGEMENT

Below is a check list of in-class teacher behaviours that I regard as vital for effective classroom management. Practice of these attitudes and behaviours will certainly lead to a major decrease in classroom difficulties and also act as a means of preventing other problems developing.

Checklist of Positive In-Class Teacher Behaviours

1. Unconditional relationship with each student
2. Recognition of the influence of self-esteem on learning
3. Sees person and behaviour as separate issues
4. Knows that learning is not an index of capability
5. Views success and failure as relative terms

6. Employs mistakes and failures as opportunities for learning
7. Puts emphasis on effort rather than performance
8. Makes sure that learning has only positive associations
9. Does not project own needs onto students
10. Sees a student's problem behaviour as saying something about that student, not about the teacher
11. Stays calm and relaxed at all times
12. Is fair, consistent and predictable in responses to all students
13. Frequently praises and affirms students
14. Is positively firm in the face of difficult behaviour from students
15. Listens to all sides
16. Prepares lessons well
17. Requests rather than commands
18. Is child-centred rather than programme-centred
19. Is not trapped into conflict with student presenting maladaptive behaviour
20. Knows when help is needed

It can be seen that most of the pointers given above have already been discussed in previous chapters. This just confirms that attention to the self-esteem of both teacher and student is central to classroom management. A few of the behaviours (4, 14, 15 16, 19) need further elaboration.

A surprising revelation for me was that learning is not an index of a person's capability! Conditioning had led me to believe that genetics rather than environment was the determinant of intellectual functioning. However, research has now shown that the best predictor of intellectual functioning is socio-economic status. Only about one to two per cent of children from 'lower class' families go onto third level education compared to over twenty per cent of 'middle-class' families. It is hardly the case that the former have less capability than the latter. The difference is in opportunities. Middle-class children come from homes where sensory stimulation is qualitatively and quantitatively high, one-to-one verbal encounters are frequent, education is highly valued, children are encouraged to talk, read and constructively play, parents themselves are often still in pursuit of further education and children are more motivated to learn. The level of knowledge and motivation to learn of these latter children is far greater by the time they come to the primary school and puts them at a distinct advantage over children who come from 'disadvantaged' situations. However, the child's level of scholastic response often becomes the determinant of academic labelling of children on a range from highly intelligent to mentally handicapped. Labels in turn determine teachers' expectations of children and when a child self-labels (internalisations of labels from significant adults), (s)he or tends to live up or down to that label. For example, children who believe they are 'poor readers' read poorly. Many adults have labelled themselves in terms of intellectual activities. Most adults believe they are useless at public speaking or voicing questions in a group and they generally fulfil their own prophecies. Many adults believe they are 'no good at mathematics' and dread any public exposure to mathematical questions. However, I have no doubt that each person has the capacity to comprehend any branch of knowledge given belief in self, application and appropriate learning opportunities. What a boost to a child's self-esteem is the communication "you are immensely capable" and your present level of knowledge is no index of your capabilities as a person. **Knowledge is peculiar to cultures not to intelligence**. For example, the Aborigine people whilst having extremely poor verbal functioning, compared to people in western society, have highly developed and advanced right brain hemisphere functioning in terms of visual, spatial and mechanical abilities. It is important therefore that teachers do not confuse knowledge with capability. Teaching is about increasing children's knowledge; you cannot increase a child's intellectual capability.

Item 14 in the list above recommends that the teacher be positively firm in the face of a child's under-control behaviour. This also links up with item 19 of the checklist which advises not to get into conflict with a student who is out of control. The issue here is that aggression breeds aggression and that negative responding on a teacher's part to a student's maladaptive actions will only escalate the situation. Indeed, if possible, the best strategy is to give no attention to the student (as often the sub-conscious ploy is to gain attention). The no attention response often defuses the student's under-controlled reactions. If a response has to be shown it is essential that the teacher stay calm and in self-control and firmly, but positively, request the student to desist from the unacceptable behaviour. There is little chance of the latter if the teacher loses control of self. Furthermore, the teacher's loss of control gives the student control over the teacher and further licence to engage in his or her disruptive responses. Sometimes no matter what the teacher does the student may persist in the maladaptive behaviours. Possible strategies in such a situation are discussed in section 8 of this chapter.

The other two items (15 and 16) not discussed in previous chapters nearly speak for themselves. Listening is the first and, indeed, most important act in communication. Children need to be both heard and seen. Fo example, frequent enquiries of students regarding any difficulties they might be having with your subject(s) will often prevent future accusations of unfairness or of not understanding sections of the course. It certainly will communicate your concern for them and willingness to listen to their side. In conflict situations be wary of judging too quickly; listen to all sides before making a final assessment of what has transpired.

6. DESIGNING A SYSTEM OF STUDENT RESPONSIBILITY

Traditional discipline systems tended to stress the 'do nots' demanded within school and class systems. Such an approach does not demonstrate to students 'what to do' and hence does not foster a student's own self-control and responsibility within the school. The word 'discipline' has many negative associations for many of us who came through school systems and I much prefer to use the phrase 'educating for responsibility'. In designing a system of responsibility within and outside the classroom, a list of the key responsibilities of students needs to be drawn up by a committee which has management, principal, vice-principal, teacher, student and parent representatives. It is best that such a list be kept to a minimum.

Examples of such responsibilities are:-
In-class Responsibilities
- Is on time for class
- Walks in an orderly way into class
- Sits in seat immediately
- Stays in seat
- Moves around classroom in orderly way
- Waits quietly for instructions and directions
- Hands up assigned homework
- Communicates in respectful fashion to teachers and fellow students
- Respects other people's property
- Speaks at an acceptable noise level
- Responds positively to requests from teachers
- When disturbed or angry requests personal time with teacher
- When class teacher does not respond to reasonable complaints of unjust behaviour brings issues to committee for student responsibility

Out-of-Class Responsibilities
- Walks along corridors in orderly fashion
- Respects school and other people's property
- Speaks at an acceptable noise level
- Plays in school yard in a way that is safe for others
- Communicates in respectful way to others

Students need to be frequently reminded of these responsibilities. Indeed a copy of these responsibilities and accompanying sanctions (see below) for irresponsibility should be posted in every classroom, also a copy should be sent to the parents of each child. An explanation or rationale for these responsibilities needs to be given. Such a rationale could be typed below the list of responsibilities. Guidelines for such explanations are:
- Relative quiet needed for learning to occur

- Safety of self and others
- Taking care of one's own and other's belongings
- Making the best effort
- Creation of positive teacher-student and student-student relationships

Positive Use of Sanctions

As outlined above in an earlier section any social system has to employ sanctions in order to ensure adherence to agreed responsibilities. Within a school, it is essential that sanctions be employed within a context where teachers have unconditional positive relationships with students, use positive teacher-student communication, emphasise academic effort rather than performance and clearly and consistently reinforce effort. As regards the latter how many teachers thank their children for listening and effort at the end of each class? The implementation of a sanction must be done in such a way that the student knows precisely how (s)he has been irresponsible and what exactly is required of him or her the next time. Sanctions must educate for responsibility. They must not be a means of 'putting down' children.

The positive use of sanctions has certain clear characteristics:

a) When possible, the sanction used is the **natural** result of the irresponsible behaviour. For example, if a student wastes time in class, then a natural sanction is to deprive him or her of break or leisure time. If a student in temper throws materials all over the classroom a natural sanction is to get him or her to tidy up the room.

b) Sanctions must be **predictable** and **consistent**. This means that students always know where responsibility lies and know that breaching that line will always lead to the application of a sanction. Furthermore, students need to know that no matter which teacher it is or which student chooses to be irresponsible the same sanction outcome will occur.

c) Sanctions must always be **fair** and **just**: the sanction must always fit the irresponsibility. When sanctions are agreed by a committee and not left up to the whim of a particular teacher then the possibility of injustice is considerably lessened. The suggestion that the committee frequently reviews the responsibility system also guards against injustice.

d) Sanctions must be **impersonal**: The teacher who loses his or her temper with a student who is inattentive and assigns a sanction that arises from the teacher's own projections or needs for attention will not be effective with students. The students know that the sanction is only an outlet for the teacher's dependency and they blame him or her rather than themselves.

e) Sanctions must emphasise **what is expected** of students so that they become an opportunity for more responsible behaviour and self-control.

f) Sanctions should be **withheld** until the teacher understands the **psychological 'rightness'** of the maladaptive behaviour and assigns the sanction in a way that clearly demonstrates that understanding.

g) Sanctions must be **positively and calmly applied** so that the student does not become fearful of the teacher. Fear blocks the communication path between student and teacher. Furthermore, a student who is frightened may agree to anything, but when he recovers, (s)he will have learned nothing and his or her next act of irresponsibility may be worse than the first.

h) Sanctions must **never involve the assignment of 'lines' or extra homework**. This refers back to a earlier point that learning must only have positive associations for students.

i) The **student's first name** must always be used in assigning a sanction.

What sanctions are available for use within a school system? Different social systems demand different solutions and each school needs to determine the best responsibility system for its unique culture. Therefore the list below is just a general guideline.

List of available sanctions for schools

- Positive and firm requests for responsible behaviour
- Withdrawing attention from irresponsible action (this very often is effective as the ploy can be to get teacher attention).
- Deprivation of privileges
  (the possible loss of an activity that a student thoroughly enjoys becomes a strong motivation for responsibility).
- Detention with a meaningful purpose
  (this needs to be supervised and the supervisor needs clear directions on what academic task has been assigned to the student); this task could be, for example, completion of class and homework not done but not extra 'punishment' assignments.
- Non-academic duties during break-times eg. collecting litter
- Warnings of being sent to a) class teacher (peculiar to second levels schools) and b) to vice-principal or principal.
- Placement in a lower class (most students hate this because their irresponsibility becomes public knowledge to a younger peer group they might want to impress).
- Being on report
  (many schools now employ a report-card system which teachers are required to mark at the end of each class).
- Being sent to a) class teacher or b) vice-principal or c) principal
- Letter to parent(s)
- Meeting with parents
  (It is advisable that both parents be invited in to discuss their child's progress in school).
- Written warning of suspension given to student and sent to parents.

- Suspension
- Expulsion
  (This is a last resort where the needs of the teacher(s) and students outweigh that of the student who is recalcitrant or who needs more specialised education or psychological or social help.

7. IMPLEMENTATION OF STUDENT RESPONSIBIL- ITY SYSTEM

The effective implementation of an agreed system of responsibility depends on the **full co-operation** of all teachers with strong back-up from principals, vice-principals, management boards and parents. Within the school **predictability** and **consistency** across all teachers for all students and within each setting are paramount. Any break in cither of these factors weakens the system and allows students to play off one teacher against another or one situation against another. The context of **close relationships with students, belief in students' capability** and emphasis on and **frequent reinforcement of academic effort** must be maintained at all times. Such a school environment not only prevents the development of many problems but makes it easier to correct irresponsibility when it does occur.

Better commitment to an agreed system arises from the inclusion of all parties in the design of the system. The formation of a committee who are responsible for monitoring and reviewing the system is important. Again such a committee is best comprised of representatives from the various groups: teachers, students (except in the case of very young children) parents and management. **The decisions of this committee must not be overruled** by any one teacher or principal. The latter would have the effect of weakening the power of the committee and of the system of responsibility. One of the major functions of the committee would be to arbitrate on the 'grey' areas of what a particular responsibility or sanction precisely means. Different responsibilities may mean different things to different students and teachers. When either a student or teacher needs clarification on an issue (whether it be a particular responsibility or sanction) then redress to the committee should be made. Its decision must be the final one.

8. RESPONDING TO A STUDENT WHO IS RECALCITRANT

Even after a teacher has developed a positive classroom atmosphere through close relationships with students, has made lessons as interesting and student-centred as possible, is relaxed and calm in teaching, allows students to constructively voice their needs, grievances or worries and has led students to a reasonable level of self-control, (s)he may find himself or herself faced with a student showing under-control behaviours. The under-control behaviours that distress most teachers are aggressive outbursts or insulting verbal behaviour from students. The tendency is to react negatively to a display of such behaviours and, unfortunately, such a response will only escalate the student's problematic actions.

It is wise for teachers to be aware that aggressiveness or insolence on a student's part inevitably arises from the hidden need to be loved, valued and accepted and is preceded by some experience during which the student felt hurt, angry or frightened. When the student has 'cooled down' the teacher should give the student a normal amount of affection and safety and attempt to discover what hurt, angered or frightened him or her. Even though some sanction may still need to be imposed it can be done now within the context of this understanding. Indeed, the teacher may find that (s)he needs to change some aspect of his or her behaviour towards the student.

Nevertheless, when a student exhibits out of control behaviour some immediate action is needed in order to diffuse the situation. **Sometimes the best action is no action**. Verbally confronting an out of control student rarely works (even though the teacher may do it in a positive but firm way) as the student is highly emotionally upset and requests for reasonable behaviour are likely to fall on deaf ears. There is nothing better than hurt, anger or fear to deafen a student to the voice of reason. Emotion in this context is always stronger than cognition . The no action response to the student and the encouragement of the rest of the class to continue the given academic activity takes the focus off the distressed student and because behaviour always has the function of eliciting a response it can quickly extinguish when no reaction is forthcoming. If the latter happens then no reference to the student's maladaptive behaviour must be made during the remainder of the class. However, at the end of the class, it is important that the teacher takes some private and personal time with the student so that they can jointly discover what led to the problematic behaviour. This may require requesting a colleague to cover your next class for a short period of time.

When a student's behaviour puts the teacher or other students at risk then some decisive action is required. When other students are at risk the teacher needs to quietly and calmly request the class to leave the classroom and assemble in an orderly way in a designated place. Also, request one of the more responsible students to relay what is happening to the principal and ask the principal to take responsibility for your class in the meantime. Do not physically approach the student but stay at a distance, silent and calm.

When a student physically attacks the teacher it is essential that the teacher does not retaliate as all hell will then break loose. (S)he should calmly back away from the student, maintaining strong eye contact (so that the student sees that the teacher is in control), request the class to leave as above and send a student for immediate back-up from the nearest teacher.

No matter what the situation is, analysis of the event must take place afterwards in a secure setting for both pupil and teacher. A useful way to analyse maladaptive behaviour is by means of an ABC system:

ABC Analysis of Maladaptive Behaviour

A stands for antecedent: what went on before the onset of the problematic behaviour, whether between the teacher and student, or student and peer, or some event prior to coming into class or prior to coming into school. Other possible antecedents may be covert such as aggressive thought patterns or 'bottled-up' resentments. Very often it is these external or internal events that trigger the student's maladaptive behaviours. When these are isolated a clearer picture is revealed and the teacher may discover that it was his or her negative language that offended the student or the student may discover that it was his or her own 'nursing' of unresolved hurts that led to the outburst. In either case something can be corrected so that these triggers are removed from social interactions. Sometimes it may be some aspect of the classroom setting that acts as a trigger, for example, over-hot room, being seated next to the student who bullies or teases, or inadequate equipment for assigned project.

B stands for behaviour: what precisely has the student done, whether it is the use of foul language, or refusal to carry out an assignment or inattentiveness in class. The more clearly the behaviour is defined then the easier it is to define the responsibility that the student will be expected to take on as part of the resolution of the conflict. In the examples given above, the clear responsibilities are appropriate communication of needs, acceptance of class assignments and application to classwork.

C is for consequences: what follows the behaviour. For example, very often students' academic efforts, politeness, caring for property go unnoticed leading to extinction of such responsible behaviours. Reinforcement of responsible behaviours is not frequent enough within most homes and classrooms. There are different types of reinforcers - social, tangible, token - and when these are given contingent on efforts to be responsible they lead to an increase in such behaviours. Social reinforcers (praise, pat on the back, affirmation, encouragement, smile...) are the most powerful of all. Token reinforcers include points, credits, stars, money; all of which can be converted to tangible or activity reinforcers. You have seen that when the consequence to a student's aggression is aggression then this serves only to increase the student's maladaptive behaviour. However, if the consequence is no attention at all to the aggressive behaviour, then this often leads to an extinction or reduction of that behaviour.

By examining the three phases of a sequence of behaviour much can be learned about what needs to be changed at both the antecedent and consequence stages in order to bring about a change at the behavioural level. The above analysis is certainly helpful in the immediate situation but it does not isolate the deeper affective issues of why one student reacts more aggressively or hypersensitively than another student. Such issues may only emerge on acquiring a deeper insight into the pupil's internal and external life. You have already seen what many of these issues may be; the most common being a dysfunctional, unhappy home situation, undue pressure for academic and general performance and low self-esteem. Finally, the more extreme are the student's maladaptive behaviours the more serious are the hidden issues of abusive home situations and low self-esteem.

When a student persists in engaging in irresponsible behaviour, in spite of the teachers' and others' best efforts to help the student then some outside intervention is required. Clearly, if the child has a learning difficulty then some special teaching for learning difficulties may be the option needed. A note of caution here is that many children's poor intellectual functioning arises from deeper affective problems and when the latter are resolved children begin to academically thrive. Therefore, any assessment of a child needs to be **holistic** so that all aspects of his or her life are examined. Some children who are problematic come from a sub-culture where the values, morals, attitudes and standards of behaviour are very different to that of the school. The attempt here is to impose the 'majority' culture onto this child, who, inspite of his or her best efforts may 'feel out of things'. A school more suited to a child's sub-culture would be more appropriate for such a student. Moreover, there is a certain disrespect in imposing your own culture onto another person of a different culture. Other students exhibiting persistent difficulties may require individual counselling or psychotherapy but preferably family therapy. When parents become involved in the resolution of their child's conflicts speedy progress can be made. It is important to recall here that sometimes it is the teacher who requires psychological help.

Early detection and intervention for students displaying socially unacceptable behaviour within the school and classroom are essential. Too often problems are allowed run too long before positive and decisive action is taken. Other students and teachers should not have to tolerate disruption in classes over a long period of time. Control difficulties have become a major cause of burnout in teachers and resolution of these issues must occur within each school, with the back-up of psychological and social services as well as support and resource allocation from the Department of Education.

9. USE OF BACK-UP PROFESSIONAL SERVICES

It is clear that many of the problems of children are either emotional or social in origin and that these children and their families require help from agencies offering psychological and social help. Traditionally there has been an intellectual and learning assessment psychological service available to schools but this has been too narrow in its focus to be able to resolve students' emotional and social difficulties. Furthermore, there are teachers who need psychotherapeutic help and such a service needs to be made available in a highly confidential context. Many schools have no back-up help services and teachers are left floundering as to what to do with children in distress. A confrontative style of management (see Chapter 6, Section 3) is needed to demand the development and availability of these services. Teachers are not psychologists nor social workers nor family therapists. Many career guidance teachers, whose role has been greatly pared-down because of financial cut-backs, are loaded with trying to help such children. Again, this is not their brief and neither has their professional training equipped them to deal with such children. Some career guidance teachers, to their credit, and at their own expense, have done various counselling or psychotherapy or family therapy courses. Whilst this is laudable it does mean that the Department of

Education is somewhat left off the hook to provide in-school student counselling services. There is certainly the beginnings of movement towards providing more comprehensive back-up services to schools. Indeed, it is in the interests of the Departments of Education and Health to provide such services, as early detection and intervention will mean that children in distress will not later become clients of adolescent and adult psychological and social services.

Deciding whether a student's difficulties require specialised attention is not necessarily as easy as might be assumed. Emotional and social signs of disturbance are, by and large, exaggerations, deficits and debilitating combinations of behaviour patterns common to all children. The following are the main factors to consider before a decision is made as to whether or not the problems of a student need specialised professional intervention.

When to refer a student for specialised help

a. Age and the stage of the child's development

Whether or not many problems are considered in need of professional help will depend on the student's age. Behaviours which are common and normal at some ages are maladaptive at others. For example, temper tantrums are common in pre-school children and hence 'the terrible two's'. Enuresis (bed-wetting) occurs frequently in children up to the age of three or four years but is clearly maladaptive in a children of over five years and even more alarming in an adolescent. Younger children have many fears, only because they are still becoming acquainted with many aspects of their world. However, school-going children and adolescents manifesting fears of the dark or of failure, or of conflict, or of other students, are clearly manifesting hidden emotional or social conflicts.

b. Frequency

The more frequently a behavioural difficulty is occurring then the more likely it is that specialised attention is needed. An odd occurence may only indicate a transient difficulty which clears up with the passage of time and life experience.

c. Intensity

The more extreme the emotional intensity (extreme anger, panic, timidity) and avoidance or aggressive behavioural patterns then the higher the indicators are that this student (or teacher!) needs help. For example, about one-third of children show reluctance in going to school, but a child who has developed a phobia of school will exhibit severe distress and panic feelings when attempts are made to bring him or her to school. Excessive distress will manifest itself in the child's physiological state (increased heart rate, paling, vomiting, stomach pains, trembling, etc.), in verbally expressed feelings of fear and discomfort and attempts to avoid or escape from school.

d. Persistence

This has already been alluded to in a previous section. The more for example, aggression, tantrums, non-cooperation, fears, phobias, timidity, bed-wetting, soiling, withdrawal, depression, sadness persist over a long period of time then the greater the indicators are for immediate referral to appropriate back-up services. Many adolescents who display persistent difficulties are carrying problems from childhood which, regrettably, were not picked-up at that stage of development. Secondary difficulties will also have developed for these adolescents as scholastically and socially they now will often have fallen far behind their peers, leading to yet another blow to their self-esteem.

e. Student's Home Environment

It has been my experience in working with some referred children and adolescents that it is their parents who need help and not the children. Very often I do little to treat the children but put great emphasis on changing the parents' relationship with the child. Many parents project their own insecurities, unmet needs, perfectionism, rigidities, anxieties, pessimism and helplessness unto children and unless these problems are resolved the children of those parents will continue to be at risk. The maladaptive behaviour of children can be a normal response to an abnormal situation. The abnormality resides in the environment rather than in the child. For example, aggressive responses in a student may be the consequences of that student's modelling or imitating parental behaviour. Alternatively, the student's aggression may be a function of the blocking of his or her needs within a rigid, restrictive, dominating and controlling family code of behaviour. Furthermore, problems of theft, delinquency and truancy in adolescents have been associated with parental attitudes of indifference. In these latter circumstances the child or adolescent, finding no security in the home, will often seek acceptance from his or her peer group and follow the norms of that group. Within the group, activities such as truancy, theft and aggression might be normal: yet another example of the influence of the environment rather than pathology within the young person.

f. Students' School and Classroom Environments

All the indications are that not all problems of children arise from their family circumstances, but a school environment or a particular teacher's behaviour may explain why a child is experiencing some emotional and behavioural difficulties. You have already seen how a child from a sub-culture may not 'fit-in' to a school environment with a very different culture. This child needs placing in a more appropriate school environment to meet his or her particular needs. There are teachers who have their own deep emotional difficulties and these may manifest themselves through, for example, aggression, controlling, dominating, cynicism, sarcasm or timidity, fearfulness and anxiety within the classroom, leading to difficulties for students. As in the case of parents in the examples above, it is the teachers who need professional help and not the student. Many school principals have difficulty in approaching these teachers and some confidential system is needed that principals could employ in such situations. Sometimes it is the school principal who is problematic and it is important that teaching staff have some means of relaying concerns and worries to an effective source.

Most students who are referred for specialised help are reacting with maladaptive behaviour to traumatic home or school life experiences in the present or past. As such, the help of choice should be psychotherapy or family therapy. Drug treatment is not to be recommended. The latter thirty years have seen the emergence of a variety of helping methods: behaviour therapy, cognitive therapy, gestalt psychotherapy, client-centred psychotherapy. These latter approaches either attempt to change the environment a child lives in or deal directly with the child's emotional and behavioural difficulties. Family therapy has also developed and this involves treating the whole family and seeing some dysfunction within the system as the source of a child's difficulties.

These treatments are often effective and the high demands for them are indicative of that effectiveness. Finally, it is my conviction that an understanding of the student's inner life and of that of his parents and teachers too, must always precede the choice of therapeutic approach.

10. KEY ISSUES

- Classroom control is the responsibility of students

- It is a recipe for conflict to get one person to control another

- The teacher has the responsibility to retain control of himself or herself

- When a teacher loses control of self (s)he gives the students control over him or her.

- Classroom management is about educating children to take responsibility for themselves.

- Giving responsibility to students and believing in their ability to meet it are powerful boosts to their self-esteem.

- Persistent emotional and behavioural difficulties of students arise from either deficiencies in the process of socialisation or excessive pressure inside or outside the child.

- It is problems of under-control that mostly disrupt learning within classrooms.

- Knowing that a student who is problematic has a difficult home situation is no justification for saying 'nothing can be done'.

- Children with emotional and behavioural difficulties respond positively to a school and classroom environment wherein they are consistently loved, valued, affirmed, encouraged and praised.

- Students' problems can also arise from factors within the school and classroom.

- There are positive in-class teacher behaviours that promote a healthy classroom environment.

- Knowledge is not an index of intelligence.

- Aggression breeds aggression.

- Listening is the first act of communication.

- A system of student responsibility within and outside the classroom should be devised by representatives of all parties involved.

- A rationale for student responsibilities needs to be provided.

- Sanctions must educate for responsibility.

- Predictability and consistency are the hallmarks of an effective system of responsibility within a classroom and school.

- The decision of a committee for student responsibility must not be overruled by any other teacher or school principal.

- Aggression or insolence on a student's part arises from a hidden need to be loved, valued and accepted and is preceded by some experience during which the student felt hurt, angry or frightened.

- Hurt, anger and fear deafen students to the voice of reason.

- An ABC analysis of a distressing incident reveals immediate remedial actions that can be taken.

- When problems persist, in spite of the best efforts of teachers and others, outside professional help is needed.

- Early detection and intervention for students displaying maladaptive behaviours is important for the student, other students, the teachers and the school.

- Back-up psychological and social services are needed for students and teachers displaying persistent problematic behaviours.

- Treatments of choice are psychotherapy and family therapy.

11. KEY TASKS

- Stay calm, relaxed and in control of self at all times.

- Frequently remind students of their classroom responsibilities and the sanctions for irresponsible behaviours.

- Let students know that the choice of being responsible or irresponsible lies with them and it is they who choose an assigned sanction.

- Avoid the use of inappropriate behaviours that damage students' self-esteem.

- Arrange professional help for your own emotional difficulties.

- Avoid getting into conflict with a student who is exhibiting under-control difficulties.

- Listen to all sides.

- Display list of student responsibilities within each classroom.

- Apply sanctions in a way that demonstrates understanding of the underlying difficulties of students.

- Be predictable and consistent in your responses to students' maladaptive behaviours across all students and all situations.

- Sometimes the best action is no action.

- Jointly (teacher and student) explore what underlies the student's disruptive actions.

- When needed, ask for support and help from colleagues: remember this is a two-way street.

CHAPTER SIX

The School

1. **THE EFFECTIVE SCHOOL**

   - High Expectations
   - Emotional Responsiveness

2. **EFFECTIVE LEADERSHIP**

   - Main Characteristics
   - Style of Leadership
   - Role-Model
   - Time-Management
   - Blocks to Effective Time-management
   - Delegation
   - Blocks to Delegation
   - Relating to Staff

3. **COPING STRATEGIES WITHIN SCHOOLS**

   - Conforming Coping Style
   - Confrontative Coping Style

4. **WHOLE-SCHOOL APPROACH**

   - Shared Responsibility
   - Predictability and Consistency

- Effective Communication
- Staff Support and Development
- School Identity

5. INVOLVEMENT OF PARENTS

- Parents of pupils presenting classroom problems
- Parents as Educators
- Training of Parents
- Parents on School Committees
- Parents as Resources

6. KEY ISSUES

7. KEY TASKS

1. THE EFFECTIVE SCHOOL

All the indicators are that an effective school has characteristic patterns of behaviour revolving around three main themes: high expectations of students and staff, emotional responsiveness and effective leadership. The first two themes involve interactions that lead to the elevation of self-esteem of both students and teachers. The high expectations exhibit a belief in students' and teachers' immense capacity to learn and to cope with all aspects of life. The emphasis is on effort, not performance, and students and teachers are frequently affirmed and encouraged in their academic, social, behavioural and emotional efforts. Mistakes and failures are seen as opportunities for further development. Children are not academically compared to each other as each child is seen as a unique human being possessing his or her own special way of perceiving and interacting with the world. Teaching is also child-centred and works from a child's present level of attainment. All efforts are seen as attainments and feedback on scholastic work is given in such a way that the student knows precisely where his or her next academic efforts need to be focused. Teachers themselves are encouraged to affirm their own uniqueness and efforts. They too employ mistakes and failures as stepping stones to further academic knowledge and understanding of human behaviour. There is a sharing of knowledge and experience among teachers and requests for help in teaching a particular subject are actively encouraged. Children are also encouraged to seek help when needed. Learning and study have only positive associations.

Emotional responsiveness is concerned with the creation of unconditional valuing relationships between teacher and teacher, teacher and student, principal and staff, student and student and teachers and parents. The uniqueness of each person within the school system is emphasised and respected. Affirmation, warmth, praise, encouragement, support and comfort, are frequent features of the inter-relationships between all members of the system. The development of close relationships and support networks are key issues. There is an absence of any behaviour that damages the self-esteem of anyone within the system such as destructive criticism, comparisons of one person with another, ridiculing, scolding, cynicism and sarcasm. At the same time, any behaviour that is disrespectful of anyone within the system is firmly responded to and appropriately agreed sanctions are assigned. Open, relating communication is taught and practised; beginning with principal and teachers who act as models for students. Feelings are seen are barometers of the present emotional state of a person and emergency feelings are seen as indicators of conflicts that need resolution. Responsibility for self is clearly laid on the shoulders of each teacher and student and any attempt to slide out of responsibility is firmly confronted. At all times a clear distinction is made between person and behaviour. When confrontation on maladaptive behaviours (whether of students or teachers) is made, the focus is on behaviour and the maintenance of the relationship is seen as essential for the resolution of the conflict issue. Listening is seen as essential.

A school environment that provides such emotional responsiveness, responsible permissiveness, support, understanding, compassion, unconditionality and positive firmness leads to the elevation of each person's self-esteem within the system. This, in turn, brings about further emotional maturity on the part of each person and an expanding cycle of physical, psychological and social wellness develops. The converse produces a cycle of distress. The involvement of parents is seen as essential as they are actively encouraged to back-up the school system and to create a similar environment in the home (see section 5 below).

The third characteristic of the effective school is effective leadership. Mature leadership is a crucial issue within any system. When parents have low or middle self-esteem problems then they will have many deficits in emotional maturity, communication, problem-solving, expression of feelings, independence and closeness and inevitably the family system suffers. So too with other organisations. The insecure, low to middle self-esteem leader inevitably undermines the self-esteem of those below him or her in the organisation leading to a dysfunctional system. The characteristics of effective leadership are discussed in the following section.

2. EFFECTIVE LEADERSHIP

The most important characteristic of an effective school principal is high self-esteem. Such a leader will have:

- Value and belief in self and life
- Ability to unconditionally value others
- A capacity for focussed attention
- Ability to appraise teachers' and students' efforts
- Problem-solving and conflict-resolution skills

The style of leadership will entail:

- Assertiveness with regard to own beliefs and conflict issues
- Affirmation of staff and students
- Flexibility in the face of difference
- Internal control and independence
- Challenging of self, staff and students
- Tolerance of mistakes, failures and vulnerability
- Responsiveness to all expressed feelings by staff and students
- High expectation of staff and students in terms of academic, social and emotional efforts
- Availability
- Approachability
- Listening Skills
- Decisiveness
- Direct and clear communication
- Provision of safety and security for distressed staff or student members
- Confidentiality
- Non-conformity

The effective leader also acts as a role model for others in the system in terms of:

- Self-awareness of own strengths and weaknesses
- Self-disclosure of need for help and support

- Balanced life-style
- Close personal relationships and support systems
- Flexibility and openess to other people's differences
- Responsibility for own professional, emotional and social needs
- Hope and meaning in all aspects of life
- Direct and clear communication
- Physical fitness
- Healthy diet
- Relaxation and calmness
- Effective time-management

Many school principals find themselves overburdened with a wide variety of demands and more effective time-management and delegation of work could ease that situation for them.

Time Management Checklist
As principal do you:
- Have a daily time-management system
- Account for each hour of your work time
- Make lists of tasks to be done
- Identify priorities
- Have short, medium and long-term goals
- Realistically estimate time-allocation for tasks
- Programme only 60 per cent of your time
- Book yourself some free time
- Allow for 'travelling time' between tasks
- Adhere to your time-table
- Allocate time for making phone calls
- Use answering machine when busy
- Finish each task before going onto the next
- Revise your time-scheduling regularly

Principals who have self-esteem difficulties will find it difficult to carry out the above as they tend to be dependent on others for approval and engage in behaviours that block effective time-management.

Blocks to Effective Time-Management

As school principal do you .....

- Have difficulty in saying 'no' to demands made on you
- Give too much time to particular staff member or student
- Avoid doing things that you do not like doing
- Avoid issues that threaten your self-esteem
- Avoid confrontation on difficult issues
- Take long breaks
- Usually arrive late
- Often do useless tasks
- Frequently need someone else to check your work
- Lack office equipment needed to do a job
- Meet people socially during work time
- Have difficulty in concentrating for long periods

Delegation of Work

Many school principals have difficulties in delegation. The following questions can help to identify the areas of work that can be delegated. Make a list under each question:

- As principal what work are you **required** to do?
- What do staff members **have** to do?
- As principal what are you doing now that others could take over?
- As principal what are you doing now that colleagues might do **more effectively**?

Be sure you appreciate the workload your colleagues have before delegating further work. Most importantly, do not be afraid to ask for help and support. Effective delegation rests on your knowing full well the responsibilities each of your staff carry and assigning tasks to the person who is best fitted for them. Be sure you clearly define the task you are delegating and the level of responsibility and time allocation involved. Be available for consultation.

Blocks to Delegation

- You want to get all the credit. (This is a sure sign of insecurity and dependency).

- You know best what has to be done. (This is a 'superior' attitude arising from low self-esteem and blocks others from showing their effectiveness).
- You want things done perfectly. (This shows fear of failure and mistakes, communicates distrust to colleagues and blocks risk-taking).
- Staff should see you need help. (You are responsible for your own needs; staff are not mind-readers and it is your responsibility as manager to delegate tasks).
- Staff may not want to take on assigned tasks. (Delegation of tasks is a joint activity, initiated by the school principal but the ultimate decision as to who does what should come from the staff group).
- You want to be liked. (This mirrors dependency and low self-esteem. Ironically you will gain far more respect in being direct and clear in communication and being just and consistent. You are unlikely to be accepted if you become the 'martyr' who carries all responsibilities and never asks for help).

Relating to Staff

The chapter on the staffroom covered many of the issues on the development of positive staff relationships and staff morale: open and relating communication patterns, staff affirmation, group decision-making, availability, approachability, understanding the nature of a staff member's rigidity and responding effectively to it. The main issue here is to check how you relate to colleagues. Good social skills, effective active listening and assertiveness are essential aspects of positively relating to staff.

The questions listed below will help you to evaluate how well you as a principal relate to your staff. If you answer 'yes' to the questions with an asterix or 'no' to the other questions you seriously need to review your management style.

- Do you call staff members by their first names?

- Do you greet staff members when you meet them?
- Are you approachable?
- Are you available?
- Do colleagues communicate to you personal, interpersonal and professional difficulties?
- Do you ask for feedback on your management style from staff?
- Do you have an effective management style?
- Do you express your emergency feelings when appropriate?
- Do you respond compassionately to a teacher in stress?
- Do you negotiate work responsibilities with staff?
- Do you try to control or manipulate staff?*
- Are you moody, unpredictable and inconsistent?*
- Do you believe you have the sole right to make decisions?*
- Are you aware and accepting of your strengths and weaknesses?
- Do you frequently affirm and encourage colleagues?
- Are decisions made jointly by you and the staff?
- Do you confront teachers who are engaging in socially unacceptable behaviours within the classroom or staffroom?
- Do you tend to brush difficult issues under the carpet?*
- Are you independent of staff's opinion of you?
- Do you make difficult decisions when you have to?

3. COPING STRATEGIES WITHIN SCHOOLS

There are many aspects of the educational system and of particular school and classroom systems that are dysfunctional leading to students feeling anxious, hurt, angry, rebellious and teachers feeling pressurised, fearful, aggressive, burnt out and principals and vice-principals feeling overburdened with multiple responsibilities, trying to motivate a demoralised staff and lacking basic back-up services such as secretarial and maintenance assistants. Many principals and teachers adapt to dysfunctional systems, saying "you have to work within the system" - even if it is causing many problems for individuals.

There are basically two ways teachers can react to dysfunctional systems:

- **Conforming Coping**
- **Confrontative Coping**

Conforming Coping

The confirming coping style is illustrated in Figure 1. Most teachers accept that there are many issues both in the theory and practice of education that need to change. The extent of those changes will vary from school to school and, for example, what works for so-called advantaged schools may not be applicable to many so-called disadvantaged schools. The general tendency is to conform to the system in place, roll up one's sleeves and do one' best. This style of coping often gains admiration and praise for teachers from parents and government bodies which serves to reinforce that coping style. It also means that the Department of Education is given more power to formulate policies without too much interference from schools. Furthermore, this style of coping does not measure the effects this system has on staff and students. They are seen as casualties of the system. **The system then is greater than the individuals within it**. But a system that results in stress, absenteeism, low morale, low self-esteem, burnout, psycho-somatic illnesses in staff-members, and anxiety, maladaptive be-haviours, absenteeism, low self-esteem, school drop-out in stu-dents must be dysfunctional and should not be tolerated. However, the more staff resort to conforming strategies and adapt to dysfunc-tional circumstances the greater the likelihood of the continuation of problems within the school system.

Confrontative Coping

Confrontative coping (see Figure 2) means that the person does not lie down under issues that need changing, does not accept that members of the system should become stressed and burnt out and strives for support and for solutions from both within and outside

Figure 1.

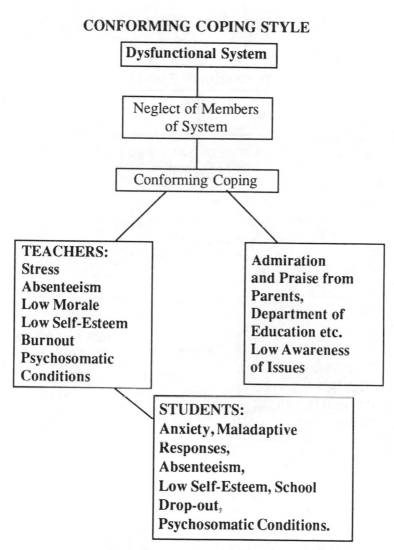

CONFORMING COPING STYLE

the school system. Most of all this coping style is person-centered rather than system-centered. When a system fails to meet the needs of individuals within it, the persons question the suitability of the system and does not blame or condemn the distressed individual (whether principal, teacher or pupil). The person coping in this way

Figure 2.

CONFRONTATIVE COPING STYLE

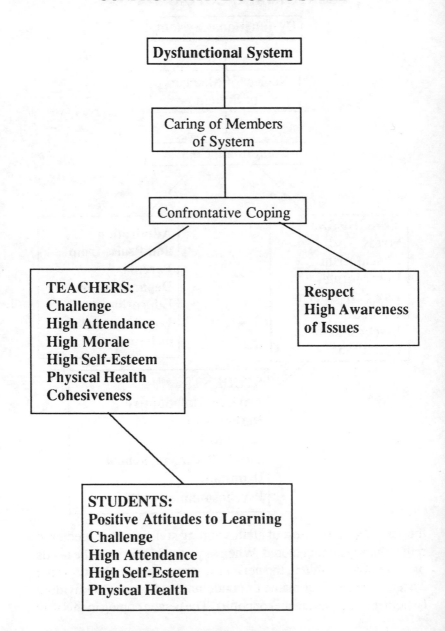

will attempt to change aspects of the system or campaign among outside bodies for the setting up of an alternative system to meet the needs of the troubled individuals. Such a style of coping means that individuals within the system feel listened to and cared for and that attempts will always be made to meet their reasonable needs either within or outside the system. The consequence then is more highly motivated staff and students who will have higher self-esteem, better physical health, high attendance and positive attitudes to learning. The morale of the school will be higher. Furthermore, such a staff will gain the respect and admiration of others and parents and officials within the Department of Education will have a greater awareness of the many issues that need to change within education.

4. WHOLE-SCHOOL APPROACH

Many of the issues involved in a whole-school approach have already arisen in earlier parts of this book. The principle underlying a whole-school approach is that of **shared responsibility**, whereby every member of the school system is involved in the development of a school environment where each person is respected, valued, affirmed, secure and safe. Staff cohesiveness is essential to the development and maintenance of such a supportive system.

No longer can teachers be left isolated in their classrooms to cope with the depth and range of emotional and behavioural problems of some students. Teachers need the back-up of the Principal and colleagues. **Predictability and consistency** across all teachers are vital for the agreed standards of behaviour to be reinforced and for breaches of that behaviour to be dealt with firmly and fairly. Teachers need very clear guidelines on how to respond to problematic behaviour within classrooms and school grounds (see section 6, chapter 5). If individual teachers operate their own classroom management systems then the likelihood of abuses of the overall system is greater.

Certainly a whole-school approach depends on effective leadership (see section 2 of this chapter) and effective communication patterns (see section 2, chapter 3). Briefly, what is needed here is a clear and well communicated management system that ensures that each member of staff knows who does what, who is responsible for each area of the school and where the lines of accountability are. Students also need to know who to go to for what, who is in charge of a particular area and what responsibilities they have within the school system (see section 6, chapter 5). A whole school approach also recognises the need for staff support systems and staff development not only in terms of academic knowledge and teaching techniques, but also awareness and practise of a greater knowledge of human behaviour within schools, homes and society in general. The latter has been a major area of neglect in teacher training. There are signs that the need for the continuing education of teachers is being recognised and that the provision of in-service courses, suitable to the culture and needs of particular schools, is on stream. There is also growing awareness of the stress and burnout within the teaching profession and awareness that a more caring environment needs to be established within schools in order to help those individuals. Teaching staffs (indeed few staffs) are noted for their understanding, compassion, caring and support. Also, the setting up of confidential counselling services for highly distressed teachers is needed. However the latter must not become an excuse that nothing can be done for that teacher within the school system. An individual teacher may derive a lot of benefit from psychotherapy, but if (s)he has to return to a non-supportive school environment, it is unlikely that the personal gains made will be maintained.

Finally, the identity of a school is an important aspect of a whole-school approach. The stronger, more dynamic and unique a school's identity the greater the loyalty and commitment of teachers and students. They feel proud to be members of such a unique system. The creation, maintenance and further development of such an identity is the responsibility of all members of this system. There is a whole range of issues in the creation of a school's identity:

- Clear and dynamic goals
- Visible and creative display of school name at entrance gate and hall.

- Attractive and well maintained school grounds
- Attractive interior decor
- Good maintenance of interior and exterior environment
- School games and inter-school competitions
- Display on corridor walls of teacher and student attainments
- Class photographs on walls
- Regular social functions
- Parent-teacher committees
- Evening courses for different community groups
- School plays, musicals and concerts
- Past pupils organisation
- Past teachers organisation
- School involvement in caring for socially disadvantaged
- School involvement in caring for environment
- Educational research
- School newsletter or magazine
- Teacher publications

5. INVOLVEMENT OF PARENTS

Many teachers have felt threatened by the increasing involvement of parents in education. Indeed, some teachers hate and dread teacher-parent meetings and see them as something to be got through rather than a source of help and support. Parents themselves also feel threatened by such meetings as they fear that teachers may say critical things about their son or daughter and they often blame themselves for their children's problems. Sometimes they will blame teachers which will cause defensiveness on the teacher's part and the probability of a clear analysis and resolution of the problem behaviour is then unlikely. The involvement of parents whose children are presenting difficulties within the classroom is necessary if any long term resolution is to be achieved. The earlier the consultation with parents the better. As has already been said many times, the children who are highly problematic come from problematic homes. Much can be done within the school to compensate for shortcomings within the home, but the co-operation of parents leads to a speedier change in children's behaviour. It is the same in therapy: when parents accept the need for family therapy, attend as needed, develop awareness and more effective coping and relating strategies, the more quickly a wellness cycle is created within the family. Approaching parents with the difficulties of their children demands a high degree of sensitivity to their vulnerability. Inevitably, the parents of pupils presenting with problems within the school, will themselves have self-esteem problems, be dependent and possibly be highly defensive either through aggression, manipulation or passivity. It is important that these parents do not feel in any way blamed or judged. Parents do not deliberately neglect, harm or put undue pressure on their children; the process is quite sub-conscious. Change may only occur through gently helping them to become aware of how what happens in the home has a damaging effect on their child. It is important too that parents feel valued and liked by the teacher and that (s)he affirms them for many of the positive aspects of the home setting. The teacher's approach to the parents needs to be one of concern for the mature development in all areas of functioning of their child. The parents need to hear the teacher as valuing and caring for the child and requesting their help to increase the child's coping within the school. They must not perceive the teacher as blaming or judging or labelling their child. Through regular meetings a joint approach may be developed to aid the child. Regular reviews, openness to informal consultation by phone, letter or quick "drop in" are made available to both parties. When some outside agency needs to be employed, this is done in a highly confidential way.

However, the involvement of parents needs to be wider than that of problem-solving. Parents can do much to create positive and challenging attitudes to education in the home. They can give children a love of learning. By the time children come to primary school their attitudes to learning may already have been formed. If the home was not qualitatively stimulating, if parents did not engage in one-to-one talking with the child, if they did not frequently read stories for their children and if they punished mistakes and failures, then it is unlikely the newcomer to school will have retained his or her natural curiosity for learning. Courses for parents as educators need to be established within both primary and secondary schools. They are not experts in how best they can provide for the intellectual development of their children. Teachers can provide them with that expertise. Other courses on the emotional and social development of children or the sexual development of children or the behavioural management of children or coping with adolescents could also be offered within the school setting. Conflict resolution skills, problem solving skills, effective communication skills, stress management skills and assertiveness skills could also be taught to parents. Many teachers could also benefit from participation in these courses. Indeed, their attendance with parents would create stronger ties with parents. A parents' committee could be formed to organise many of these events.

Circularising parents on developments within the school will add to their inclusion in school matters. As mentioned in the chapter on The Classroom, parent representatives should be on all major committees within the school system. Parents could also be encouraged to contribute to the School Newsletter and/or Magazine. Some parents may be available to offer assistance with activities inside and outside the school - a very under-used resource. The idea here is that parents have talents, skills, knowledge and expertise that can add considerably to the effectiveness of a school system.

6. KEY ISSUES

- High expectations, emotional responsiveness and effective leadership are the main characteristics of the effective school.

- High self-esteem is the hallmark of an effective principal.

- Time-management and delegation of work are central issues for effective leadership.

- Good social skills, active listening and assertiveness are essential aspects of positive relating to staff.

- Conforming coping style is neglectful of all members of a school system.

- Confrontative coping style means the person does not lie down under issues that need changing.

- Shared responsibility is the basic principle underlying a whole-school approach.

- Staff development and staff support systems have been major areas of neglect in schools and teacher training.

- A confidential counselling service for principals and teachers who are in distress needs to be developed.

- Schools can be the centre for many community activities.

- The involvement of parents whose children are problematic within the school is essential for long-term resolution of difficulties.

- Approaching parents with the difficulties of their children demands a high degree of sensitivity to their vulnerability.

- Parents can do much to create positive and challenging attitudes to education in the home.

- Teachers can provide parents with the expertise on how best to provide for the intellectual development of children in the home.

- Parents have talents, skills, knowledge and expertise that can add considerably to the effectiveness of a school.

7. KEY TASKS

- Principals to be positive role-models for teachers and students.

- Principals to devise an effective time-management system and identify blocks to its implementation.

- Principals to check attitudes to delegation of work.

- Principals to evaluate from check list (page 162, 163) how well they relate to staff.

- Staff to develop a climate of **shared responsibility** coupled with **consistency** and **predictability** of responses to students' problematic behaviour across all staff members.

- All to take responsibility to create a clear and well communicated management system which will aid the development of an effective whole-school approach.

- All to take responsibility for the developement of **a supportive and safe staff environment.**

- Determine the steps needed for a unique school identity.

- Close liaison with parents to be established.

- Setting up of courses within the school for 'Parents as Educators".

- Involve parents as assistants for activities in and out of school.

BIBLIOGRAPHY

Albert, Linda.
>*A Teacher's Guide to Co-Operative Discipline.*
>Minnesota: American Guidance Service, 1989.

Briggs, Dorothy Corkille.
>*Your Child's Self-Esteem.*
>Garden City, New York: Doubleday, 1967.

Canfield, Jack & Wells, Harold C.
>*100 Ways to Enhance Self-Control in the Classroom.*
>Englewood Cliffs, New Jersey:
>Prentice Hall, 1976.

Charlesworth, Edward A. and Nathan, Ronald G.
>*Stress Management, A Comprehensive Guide.*
>*to Your Well-being.*
>Corgi Books, 1987.

Dobson, Dr. Fitzgerald.
>*How to Discipline with Love.*
>New York: Rawson Associates, 1977.

Gray, Harry and Freeman, Andrea.
>*Teaching Without Stress.*
>London: Paul Chapman Publishing Ltd., 1987.

Glaser, William.
>*Schools Without Failure.*
>New York: Harper and Row, 1969.

Jarnpolsky, Gerald G., M.D.
>*Teach Only Love.*
>New York: Bantam, 1983.

Lawrence, Denis.
> *Enhancing Self-Esteem in the Classroom.*
> London: Paul Chapman Publishing Ltd. 1987.

Mason, L. John.
> *Guide to Stress Reduction.*
> Los Angeles: Peace Press, 1980.

O'Connor, Joyce and Ruddle, Helen.
> *Cherished Equally?*
> Limerick: Social Reseach Centre, N.I.H.E.
> Copies of this book may be obtained from the
> Mid-Western Health Board,
> 31-33 Catherine Street, Limerick.

Peck, M. Scott.
> *The Road Less Travelled.*
> Century Paperback Series, 1987.

Satir, Virginia.
> *Conjoint Family Therapy.*
> London's Souvenir Press, 1980.

Satir, Virginia.
> *Peoplemaking.*
> Palo Alto, California: Science and Behaviour
> Books Inc., 1972.

Stone, Lyndsey.
> *Managing Difficult Children in School.*
> Oxford: Basil Blackwell Ltd., 1990.

KEY POINTS INDEX